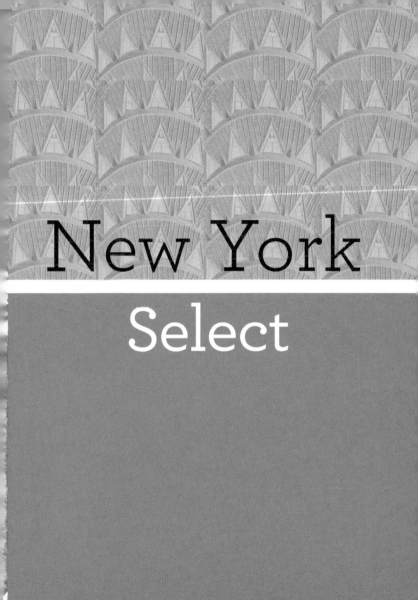

New York

Select

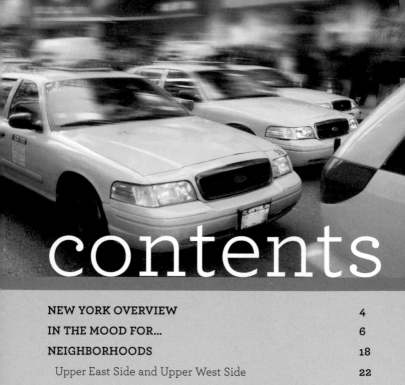

contents

New York overview

New Yorkers tend to think of their city as the center of the universe, and even if you aren't willing to subscribe to that belief, you will have to agree that New York is one of the greatest places on the planet. At least, you will feel that way after you spend any time at all here.

With its skyscrapers and sophisticated ways, the city is the essence of urbanity, just about everyone's notion of what a city should be. This is a place where dreams come true, vast fortunes are made and lost, and fame might descend briefly and flit away or linger for a spell. What all this means for visitors is that New York is a fascinating spectacle. You can see top-rate drama and great art, dine and

drink very well, and simply soak in the excitement. You might run into a celebrity on a grimy side street, or enjoy being drawn into streams of ordinary folks on the sidewalks. The city is so iconic that even visitors who have never set foot in Manhattan feel they are on familiar ground. You can look up the heights of the Empire State Building and imagine King Kong clinging to the spire or still hear Cole Porter hammering out a tune in one of the city's refined cocktail lounges.

The best way to appreciate New York is simply to throw yourself into the fray. Walk up the Upper West Side to sample bagels, amble through the galleries of the Metropolitan Museum of Art, ogle diamonds on Fifth Avenue, linger over coffee in Greenwich Village, listen to music on the Lower East Side or Brooklyn. Explore colonial New York, catch up on the contemporary art scene, ascend to the top of a tower to see the spectacle of the glittering city at your feet. However you choose to amuse yourself in this great city, you will find more to do than you have time to do it in.

in the mood for...

... street life

As the old song says, East Side, West Side, all around the town, the sidewalks of New York are a great place to trip the light fantastic – and to watch New Yorkers, some of the most fascinating specimens of life on the planet. Some especially rewarding stretches of pavement are **Union Square**, animated around the clock – on many days with shoppers poking through the stalls of the city's largest greenmarket (*p.86*). On weekends, the **streets of Soho** teem with style-hunters – both locals and the Bridge and Tunnel crowd (named for out of towners' means of egress into Manhattan), checking out high-end boutiques and each other (*p.122*). New York goes to the dogs in enclosed runs in parks like **Washington Square** (*p.105*) and **Tompkins Square Park** (*pictured, p.135*), great places to observe the antics of two- and four-legged New Yorkers. To see hipsters in their natural environment, make the trek to **Williamsburg** (*p.147*). On a walk down **125th Street** (*p.44*), Harlem's main thoroughfare, you can step into such iconic bastions of black culture as the Apollo Theater and the Lenox Lounge, and you may even run into former President Bill Clinton, one of many recent newcomers to the legendary avenue.

... fine dining

You can eat well anywhere in New York, but the settings are suitably refined and the cuisine is masterfully French-influenced in such gastronomic uptown spots as **Daniel**, **Picholine**, and **Jean Georges** (p.34) . Then again, refined French cuisine is served in sophisticated, subdued surroundings downtown, too, most notably at Bouley's, while the mouthwatering sushi at **Nobu** in Tribeca (p.128) is said to be the best this side of Tokyo, eliciting raves from celebrities and foodies alike. For some genuine New York buzz, pull up a chair at the bar of the elegant **Gramercy Tavern** in the Flatiron District (p.89) or charm your way into getting a table at the celebrity magnet **Waverly Inn** in Greenwich Village (p.104). To sample some of the most original and creative – some say bizarre – haute-cuisine in the city, head to **WD-50** on the Lower East Side (p.139).

... retail therapy

New Yorkers fall into two camps, bargain hunters and those who consider it rather crass to look at a price tag. The former are quite willing to battle the crowds at **Century 21** in Lower Manhattan or **Loehmann's** in Chelsea *(p.167)* in hopes of finding a designer original on the racks. Shoppers with an eye for vintage clothing prowl **Housing Works** and the **Angel Thrift Shop** on 17th Street in Chelsea *(p.87)*. Hipsters should head to the Lower East Side for new **designer co-op boutiques** *(p.134)*, or to the East Village for used and new **CDs, LPs and DJ equipment** *(p.144)*.

Meanwhile, those who just have to have it, whatever it costs, will find plenty of temptation on Bleecker Street from Bank to 7th Avenue in the **West Village** *(p.111)* , where the quaint, tree-lined blocks shelter such high-end designer boutiques as Marc Jacobs, Ralph Lauren, and Cynthia Rowley, and on the cobblestones of **Soho** *(p.122)*. The Upper East Side's 'if you have to ask, you can't afford it' attitude comes to the fore on **Madison Avenue** in the 60s *(p.30)*, a little patch of designer heaven where the celestial creations of Valentino, Armani and Ralph Lauren are on offer.

Fifth Avenue around 57th Street *(p.65)* is home to the city's holy trinity of refined department stores (Saks, Henri Bendel, and Bergdorf Goodman) and where the shop windows of Tiffany's, Harry Winston and Cartier are filled with glittering jewels.

... Old New York

New York is more caught up with the brash new than with the distant past, but you can get a sense of the early days of the city in such cherished landmarks as the **Morris-Jumel Mansion** *(p.49)*, Revolutionary War headquarters of George Washington and later home to Eliza Jumel and Aaron Burr – the vice-president who killed Secretary of Treasury Alexander Hamilton, who lived down the road in **Hamilton Grange** *(p.49)*. The 19th-century **Merchant's House** *(p.106)* shows off the domestic tastes of prosperous New Yorkers of a century and half ago, while uptown the **Neue Galerie** *(p.31)* and **Frick Collection** *(p.35)* show off fine art as well as the lavish homes of a long vanished era.

Thousands of enslaved men, women, and children who helped build New York from the time of the city's 17th-century Dutch days to the abolition of slavery in the US in 1865 are buried at what is now the **African Burial Ground National Memorial** *(p.162)*. Many literary giants called **Greenwich Village** home, and you can walk the streets once trod by T.S. Eliot, Ezra Pound, Edward Albee and Henry James *(p.102)*.

in the mood for...

... family fun

A fleet of historic vessels docked at the **South Street Seaport Museum** *(p.164)* are fascinating to board, and you can set sail across New York Harbor on several of them. The **American Museum of Natural History** *(p.29)* knows just how to make kids happy and just across the street is **Central Park** *(p.38)*, with its lawns, ponds, zoo, carousel and other delights. For impossible-to-please teenagers, TV comes to the rescue: a **tour of the NBC Studios** *(p.61)* – where *Saturday Night Live* and *30 Rock* are shot – will impress even the most blasé young sightseers.

... food grazing

You can eat your way through almost any New York neighborhood, but two especially rewarding foodie strips are **Ninth Avenue** *(p.75)*, lined with ethnic restaurants and markets from 59th Street to 34th Street, and Broadway on the Upper West Side, a parade of distinguished markets and delis that include **Fairway**, **Zabar's**, and **H&H Bagels** *(p.28)*. Mandatory stops on a downtown gourmet tour are **Chelsea Market** *(p.82)*, a former cookie factory now filled with fine food outlets, and **Union Square** *(p.86)*, host to the city's largest greenmarket.

... romance

Busy and brash, New York can also be one of the most romantic places on earth. You needn't spend a fortune to engage in such heartwarming follies as watching day turn to night over the Manhattan skyline from the deck of the **Staten Island Ferry** *(p.153)* or sauntering through Central Park and into the galleries of the **Metropolitan Museum of Art** (followed by a drink on the museum's rooftop sculpture garden; *p.26*). Romance is in the air even in such prosaic places as Grand Central Terminal, where you can share a Martini or two and a giant plate of oysters in the **Oyster Bar** or in the clubby confines of the **Campbell Apartment** *(p.67)*. City lights provide a romance-inducing spectacle from such hideaways in the sky as **Top of the Tower** *(p.60)*, while back on terra firma, the **King Cole Bar** *(p.69)* is one of the those plush lairs bound to sweep just about anyone off of his or her feet. Should you lose control and make a long-term commitment, the stretch of **Fifth Avenue** *(p.65)* just outside the door is lined with the world's most famous purveyors of engagement rings and other jewelry – and the **Diamond District** *(p.73)* is just down the avenue on 47th Street.

... a quintessential New York City experience

New York's landmarks never disappoint, and seeing them – even doing something as everyday as walking beneath the **Empire State Building and other Midtown towers** *(p.62)* – is one of the city's greatest thrills, even for New Yorkers. The **Statue of Liberty** always puts on a good show, and to an urbanite the skyline can be as soothing as a mountain range. You can get an eyeful of both on a walk across the Brooklyn Bridge or a ride across New York Harbor on the **Staten Island Ferry** *(p.153)*, New York icons themselves.

New York puts an innovative spin on just about everything. **The High Line** *(p.88)*, a disused railway trestle-turned-aerial park that cuts a green swath through industrial Chelsea, creates an only-in-New York twist on the great outdoors. Opera is, of course, performed in other cities, but in few places do the fat ladies sing with more finesse or are classics staged with more flair than at the **Metropolitan Opera** *(p.37)*, making a night at the opera one of the city's grandest experiences.

... being sporty

The **Chelsea Piers Sports and Entertainment Complex** *(p.90)* is New York's jock nirvana -- a sprawling 30-acre sports village on the Hudson River where you can rock climb, skate, golf, bowl, swim, or just work out. And best of all, afterwards you can sample the 20 handcrafted beers made right on the premises at the Chelsea Brewing Company.

While New Jersey is not usually associated with the word 'thrilling,' the walk there across the **George Washington Bridge** *(p.48)* certainly is, along a walkway suspended between the river and the sky. **A walk across the Brooklyn Bridge** *(p.154)* provides the same breezy experience, with a downtown perspective.

Governors Island *(p.155)* is an urban getaway where you can bike or walk along a 2-mile long waterfront promenade while absorbing views of the Statue of Liberty and Manhattan skyline; you get one hour's free bike rental on Fridays. Swimmers can plunge into **two large and stylish pools** *(p.36)* surrounded by beautiful hand-decorated Italian tiles at the West Side YMCA or the longest pool in Manhattan, a full Olympic-length 50 meters, at Asphalt Green.

... a lazy day

An easygoing day, a rare occurrence in the lives of most New Yorkers, often transpires on the tree-lined streets of **Greenwich Village**. The morning begins with a read through the papers in a laid-back coffee house over a latte and a croissant *(p.109)*. Then stroll over to the **Film Forum** for the latest foreign-language offerings, adjourn to the **Ear Inn** *(p.120)* to discuss what it all meant over a pint, and, thus mellowed, follow the picturesque streets to **St Luke's Gardens** *(p.99)* to take in some fresh air amid a beautiful botanic display.

... escaping the crowds

No man is an island, it's said, but the notion can become rather overbearing on Manhattan Island, where even a park bench can be a welcome retreat. Two especially pleasing places to sit quietly as the city swirls nearby are **Bryant Park** *(p.68)*, a tidy patch of greenery behind the New York Public Library, and the tree-shaded close of the **General Theological Seminary** *(p.81)* in West Chelsea. **The Cloisters** *(p.46)*, way uptown, provides a step back in time, to the Middle Ages, in five reconstructed cloisters where monks once found peace and you will, too.

... something free

Steep admission costs to New York City museums shouldn't keep you from enjoying some of the world's finest collections. At the **Metropolitan Museum of Art** *(p.26)* and **American Museum of Natural History** *(p.29)*, you may forgo the suggested donation and pay what you wish at any time, and you can see the **Frick Collection** *(p.35)* for the donation of your choice on Sundays from 11am–1pm. Among the many museums that offer free Friday evening admissions are **MoMA** *(p.64)*, the **New-York Historical Society** *(p.33)*, and the **Morgan Library** *(p.64)*. The **Brooklyn Botanical Garden** *(p.160)* and the **New York Botanical Garden** *(p.161)* are both free on Saturday mornings, the **Jewish Museum** *(p.33)* is free all day Saturday, and the **Brooklyn Museum** *(p.156)* is free the first Saturday of every month from 5–11pm. And for absolutely nothing, you can walk the **New York Earth Room** *(p.121)* and see a huge pile of earth covering the floor of a Soho loft – now that's something to tell the folks back home about.

... a night on the town

So many choices, so little time ... The fashion crowd gravitates to the Meatpacking District, for drinks and dinner at the **Standard Hotel**, a Parisian experience at **Pastis**, or, in warm weather, a drink on the outdoor terrace of the **Maritime Hotel** *(pictured, p.110)*. The ultimate in downtown sophistication, for the moment at least, is a cocktail in the lounge of the **Gramercy Park Hotel** followed by dinner at the refined and relaxed **Gramercy Tavern** *(p.89)*. The Lower East Side is the place for an evening of indie-rock, folk, or American roots music, and top venues are the **Bowery Ballroom** and the **Living Room**, where Norah Jones got her start *(p.136)*.

Theatergoers who would like to see a work a little more stimulating than the latest blockbuster musical should step off Broadway to **Theatre Row** *(p.70)*, home to a dozen or so small stages hosting some especially innovative drama on 42nd Street between Ninth and Tenth Avenues. Three Lower Manhattan theaters are also noted for ground-breaking work: the **Public Theater**, **LaMaMa**, and the **Wooster Group** *(p.71)*. Across the East River, the **Brooklyn Academy of Music** *(p.71)* and **St Anne's Warehouse** *(p.159)* are standard bearers of creative originality.

... literary inspirations

Washington Irving, the famous author of *Rip Van Winkle* and other magic infused fables of early America, lent his name to Irving Place, one of the most enchanting bastions of old New York. O. Henry merely drank on the street, penning some of America's favorite short stories in the dark, woody confines of **Pete's Tavern** *(p.84)*. Greenwich Village was once the city's literary Petri dish, and **literary tours** *(p.102)* show off the places where such masters of American letters as Louisa May Alcott, Edgar Allen Poe and e. e. cummings lived and wrote, and where Dylan Thomas went on his final drinking binge. You can also pay homage to the city's literary traditions in the marble hallways and Main Reading Room of the **New York Public Library** *(p.68)* – or for that matter, in the **Hotel Chelsea** *(p.80)*. Leonard Cohen found inspiration for his song 'Chelsea Hotel,' Arthur C. Clarke wrote *2001: A Space Odyssey*, and legions of other artists have found their muses or slipped into creative dissipation in this beloved monument to creativity and bohemia. The **Nuyorican Poets Café** and the **Bowery Poetry Club** *(p.142)* foster today's literary aspirants.

neighborhoods

Upper East Side and Upper West Side Central Park is the Great Divide, separating the East Side and the West Side, and this swath of greenery may as well be an ocean, so different are these two enclaves. In a nutshell, Upper Eastsiders step in and out of designer boutiques and Upper Westsiders load up on knishes at a string of delicatessens. Whatever side of the park you find yourself on, you will be surrounded by some of the world's greatest cultural institutions.

Harlem and Upper Manhattan While Manhattan took root at the southern tip of the island, much of the city's history played out north of 110th Street, and the homes of some colonial New Yorkers still stand. Uptown is bisected by 125th Street, the main street of Harlem, and is also home to one of the world's largest churches, the Cathedral of St John the Divine, and one of its greatest universities, Columbia.

Midtown The busy commercial hub of New York also displays the city's most theatrical side – literally so, on dozens of Broadway and Off-Broadway stages, and also in the neon display of Times Square and many ostentatious displays of wealth in shop windows. With its busy avenues and skyscrapers, Midtown is the essence of urbanity.

Chelsea, Flatiron, and Gramercy In relatively small geographic confines between 34th and 14th streets, New York's most schizophrenic neighborhood incorporates Little Korea, a busy gay stretch of Eighth Avenue, grimy warehouse blocks near the Hudson River, animated Union Square, a contemporary art gallery scene to the west, and a slice of Old New York in the east around Gramercy Park. Above it all floats the High Line, a railroad trestle transformed into an aerial park.

Greenwich Village and the Meatpacking District New York exudes plenty of small-town charm on the tree-shaded streets of

Greenwich Village, once home to writers, musicians, and bohemians, and now a place to sip lattes in welcoming coffee houses and walk down quaint lanes. The riverside Meatpacking District is the hip haunt of fashionistas, and the surrounding piers and shoreline have been reclaimed as a stunning park.

Soho, Tribeca, and Chinatown In New York, Downtown refers to a large swath of Manhattan beneath 14th Street. It also implies a certain level of chic style, best experienced on the cobblestone streets of Soho and Tribeca, where warehouses now house high end boutiques and places to see and be seen. A stroll east into Chinatown propels you into one of the city's thriving ethnic enclaves, yet another New York experience.

East Village, Lower East Side, and Williamsburg Time was, floods of immigrants settled on these mean streets, and they left behind synagogues, delicatessens, Russian baths, and other remnants of a way of life fondly evoked in the Tenement Museum. In their wake a new breed of immigrant has recently arrived – young hipsters who've brought with them a hopping music and club scene.

Lower Manhattan and Brooklyn
While Wall Streeters busy themselves with bailouts and sell-offs, the rest of us can board historic vessels at South Street Seaport, catch stunning sunset views of New York Harbor and the Statue of Liberty from Battery Park, and take a skinflint's cruise on the Staten Island Ferry. More diversions await in Brooklyn, and the walk there across the Brooklyn Bridge is memorable.

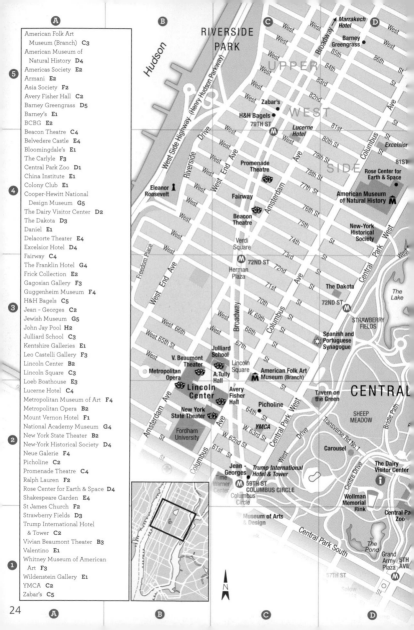

24

Upper East Side and Upper West Side

0 100 200 300 400 500 yds
0 100 200 300 400 500 m

Sip cocktails in the company of Old Masters at the **Metropolitan Museum of Art**

More than 3 million paintings and other artifacts, housed in galleries that stretch for a quarter of a mile, may not figure in your plans for a big night out on the town. But climb the monumental steps from Fifth Avenue, step into the Metropolitan Museum of Art, and you'll discover that one of the world's greatest art galleries is also one of the best places in the city to begin a weekend evening (the museum is open until 9pm on Fridays and Saturdays). Quartets play classical music, cocktails are served in romantic hideaways, and the galleries are much more navigable in the evening than they are during the day, when they can be as chaotic as Grand Central Terminal. **The Temple of Dendur**, transposed from the banks of the Nile to a stunning glass atrium overlooking Central Park, is especially atmospheric as soft twilight turns the 2,000-year-old stones golden and the trees just outside darken against the sky. The European galleries are unhurried on these evenings, so take your time to stand in front of El Greco's *View of Toledo*, Van Gogh's *Self-Portrait with a Straw Hat*, and dozens of other masterpieces so famous that they

are comfortingly familiar even to first-time visitors to the museum. Make your final stop the **Chinese Garden Court**, where the gurgle of water, graceful plantings, and an aura of serenity will restore you for whatever you're planning to do for the rest of the evening in the city swirling around you.

The Met puts on a lively roster of concerts and lectures on Friday and Saturday evenings. Check the museum's website or go to the information desk to find out what's on the evening you plan to visit. Lectures are about $23, and concerts start at $45. And on a less lofty note: it's hard to resist the Met Store, a glitzy two-floor emporium near the main entrance with an enticing array of prints, books, and distinctive jewelry and knickknacks based on the museum collections.

Metropolitan Museum of Art, Fifth Ave at 82nd St; tel. 212-535-7710, www.met.museum.org; Tue–Thur, Sun 9.30am–5.30pm, Fri–Sat 9.30am–9pm; recommended admission $20 (pay what you wish); map F4

A MUSEUM BAR CRAWL

As the saying goes, you cannot live by art alone, and you can round out an evening gallery tour with drinks and light refreshments in three exceptionally atmospheric venues within the museum. At the **Roof Garden Café and Martini Bar**, a perch high above Central Park, views extend across the sweep of greenery to the Midtown skyline (open May through late fall, weather permitting). In the **Petrie European Sculpture Court**, an excellent selection of wine is served in romantic proximity to masterworks by Rodin, Bernini, and Degas. In the **Balcony Bar**, tucked away under the arched ceiling of the Great Hall, cocktails and appetizers are accompanied by live classical music.

Nosh your way up **Broadway** for a smorgasbord of New York **gourmet delights**

Upper West Siders aren't noticeably larger than other New Yorkers, though by rights they should be, surrounded as they are by the city's most tempting delis and food markets. A culinary walk begins at **Fairway** (2127 Broadway at W. 74th St, tel: 212-595-1888, map C4), a 1930s-era fruit-and-vegetable stand turned exotic food emporium. New Yorkers, not known for saintly patience, tolerate long lines to select from 650 kinds of cheeses, 36 drums of olives, shelves stacked with store-baked bread and babka, and aisles piled dangerously high with fresh fruit and vegetables. Climb the stairs to the cafe and steakhouse for the best Reuben in town by day and aged prime rib by night.

'Like no other bagel in the world'

claims **H&H** (2239 Broadway at W. 80th St, tel: 800-692-2435, map C5), and 'We agree,' say aficionados, citing such merits as chewiness and freshness; you can buy just one, but you'll wish you'd ordered a dozen.

Zabar's (2245 Broadway at W. 80th St, tel: 212-496-1234, map C5) has prided itself on selling the finest smoked fish for 80 years, and still does – along with everything from 8,000 pounds of coffee a week, fresh-baked knishes, smoked meats, and an astonishingly large and well-priced array of pots, pans, and other gizmos for the kitchen. The next-door self-service cafe is short on decor, but lobster salad on a croissant and other offerings are so satisfying you won't mind bumping elbows with the patron on the stool next to yours.

One block east from Broadway is **Barney Greengrass** (541 Amsterdam Ave at 87th St, tel: 212-724-4707, map D5), 'the Sturgeon King.' At the city's shrine to smoked fish (and other deli classics) you can order over the counter or take a seat at a Formica table beneath dingy murals – clearly, his highness puts the emphasis on freshness, not ambience, and that's just as it should be.

Hang out with dinosaurs and **gaze at the stars** at the enthralling **Museum of Natural History**

Just looking at the American Museum of Natural History, a sprawling expanse of pink granite towers and turrets with a huge crystal cube attached, you can tell that amazing things are going on inside. And they are, from stars shooting across the night sky to giant squid floating through the depths of the ocean. No need to feel like an explorer in uncharted territory as you try to find your way through the four blocks of galleries – free Highlights Tours depart hourly to show off such prizes as the 21,000-carat Princess Topaz, a 63-foot-long canoe crafted by Pacific Northwest Indians from a single cedar tree, a 34-ton fragment of a meteorite that careened into the Greenland ice sheets. In enormous and elaborate dioramas created by taxidermists and painters in the 1940s, gorillas, lions, and other magnificent beasts range across the African rainforests and veldts; in the dinosaur halls, Tyrannosaurus rex strikes a rather terrifying stalking pose, surrounded by prehistoric companions.

One of the world's oldest natural history museums also finds flashy new ways to capture the excitement of the natural world. More than 500 butterflies flutter freely through the **Butterfly Conservatory**, undisturbed by us spectators watching from a glass tunnel (Oct–May). Cosmic collisions and other stunning extraterrestrial phenomena are earthshakingly recreated in the **Rose Center for Earth and Space**.

If you have little ones in tow, sign them up for a **Night at the Museum** (selected Friday and Saturday nights); kids 7 to 13 see an IMAX movie, tour the spookily dark galleries by flashlight, and tuck into sleeping bags beneath a 94-foot-long blue whale.

American Museum of Natural History, Central Park West at 79th St; tel: 212-769-5100; www.amnh.org; daily 10am–5.45pm; charge; map D4

Get a new look in the **glamorous boutiques** of **Madison Avenue**

Madison Avenue, especially around 65th and 66th streets, is a patch of designer heaven. In shop after shop you will mingle with wafer-thin fashionistas decked out in fabulously chic garb. We mere mortals may feel like country mice scurrying from one glamorous boutique to another, but a short walk is a fascinating foray into the world of high fashion, and you may even emerge with a new look.

Valentino (no. 747) should be your first stop if you expect to find yourself on a red carpet and wish to look your best for the paparazzi. Even if you don't have a premiere on the agenda, the glamorous gowns and tuxes will make you feel like a star.

Madison Avenue makes a sharp turn east to Milan at **Armani** (no. 760), where sumptuous limestone walls, dark wood floors and elegant staircases are as much a testament to Italian chic as the sparsely elegant attire for men and women. Attentive staffers who look like models will help you choose formal and casual designs that will ensure you fit into the surroundings.

The name says it all. **BCBG** (no. 770) stands for *Bon Chic, Bon Genre*, French for Good Style, Good Attitude. Designer Max Azria creates sexy dresses and shoes for women who have plenty of both.

A short walk north to 72nd Street, the former Rhinelander mansion is a prepster's heaven. One of the city's great Gilded Age palaces is now filled with enough **Ralph Lauren** (no. 867) tweed and plaid to clothe armies of country gents and ladies. Even if your tastes don't run to duck-emblazoned khakis, stop by for an amusing look-see: to borrow a term from the country club set, the over-the-top horse and houndish environs are 'an absolute hoot.'

The department store for style slaves of all ages, **Barney's** (no. 660) stocks all the latest top designer lines, from traditional to trendy to trashy.

Madison Avenue, map E1–F2

Enjoy some *fin de siècle* art and **sacher torte**

New York often seems to have more in common with the continent across the Atlantic than it does with the one that stretches for almost 3,000 miles from the western banks of the Hudson River. European ambience is especially pervasive in the **Neue Galerie**, a 1914 Beaux-Arts mansion that would fit right in on Vienna's Ringstrasse.

Early 20th-century socialites Cornelius and Grace Vanderbilt lived and entertained in the paneled salons overlooking Central Park, and they would probably be pleased to see them now filled with stunning early 20th-century German and Austrian paintings and decorative arts. Few enclaves in New York are more transporting, and all that slightly decadent Germanic art is especially warming on a rainy New York afternoon.

A shimmering gold-flecked portrait of Adele Bloch-Bauer by Gustav Klimt is the gallery's *Mona Lisa*, an ornate dazzler that evokes *fin de siècle* Vienna and carries a dramatic provenance to match – the early death from meningitis of the wealthy subject, confiscation by the Nazis in World War II, a protracted court battle to return the painting to the rightful heirs, and a price tag of $135 million; this sum makes the piece the most expensive painting ever sold – to billionaire Ronald Lauder, who assembled this stunning collection with famed art dealer Serge Sabarsky.

Should Adele and works by Egon Schiele, Oskar Kokoschka, and other devotees of Art Nouveau and the Bauhaus leave you in the mood to linger over a coffee and sacher torte, sink into a plush banquet in the **Café Sabarsky**.

Neue Galerie, Fifth Ave and E. 86th St; tel: 212-628-6200; http://neuegalerie.org; Thur–Mon 11am–6pm; charge; map F4

Covet the **antiques and fine art** in the exclusive galleries of the **Upper East Side**

The Downtown art scene gets all the buzz, but the solidly Blue Chip Upper East Side, wrapped securely in a mantle of wealth and social status, doesn't really give a damn. The neighborhood's understated 'if you have to ask, you can't afford it' approach is in evidence at the many art galleries and antiques houses that introduce you to New York at its most rarefied.

Gagosian (980 Madison Ave, tel: 212-744-2313, map F3) may as well be an extension of the nearby Whitney Museum, filled as the galleries are with works by Jeff Koons, Damien Hirst, and every other megastar of the contemporary art world. The **Leo Castelli Gallery** (18 E. 77th St, tel: 212-249-4470, map F3), founded by the most influential American art dealer of the 20th century, was the first to sell Andy Warhol's Campbell Soup cans, and has been on the cutting edge ever since. The sumptuous 1930s limestone **Wildenstein Gallery** (19 E. 64th St, tel: 212-879-0500, map E1) is a monument in itself, as befits the collection of Old Masters inside. Should you be in the need of a Florentine Renaissance or French Impressionist, set your sights on these four floors of hushed refinement. The well-appointed rooms at **Kentshire Galleries** (700 Madison Ave, tel: 212-421-1100, map E1) are furnished with 18th- and 19th-century British furniture that looks like it belongs in an English country house, and will make you wish you had one to furnish.

MANHATTAN MANSION

If your appetite for polished antiques has been whetted, walk east to the **Mount Vernon Hotel Museum and Garden** (421 E. 61st St, tel: 212-838-6878, Tue–Sun, 11am–4pm, charge, map F1), the remains of the estate that Abigail Adams Smith, daughter of the second US president, and her husband built in 1796. The stone house, one of the oldest in Manhattan, is beautifully furnished with early 19th-century antiques. If you're feeling a bit glum that a single piece of art or one of the antiques you've been ogling costs more than you'll make in a lifetime, take comfort in the misfortune of others – the Smiths went broke and had to sell the place.

Get a closer look at **New Yorkers and their worlds** at two idiosyncratic museums

You can't spend too much time in New York without noticing that New Yorkers are ... well, hard to sum up in one short, snappy phrase. New York is, after all, the most American of cities, founded by the earliest colonials, and the landing pad for wave after wave of immigrants. Two idiosyncratic museums provide a glimpse into this cosmopolitan and complex world and may add a bit of perspective to what you observe on the city streets.

At the **Jewish Museum**, you will encounter plenty of weighty artifacts, such as a stone from a 1st-century wall erected in Jerusalem to repel Roman invaders, alongside sound and video clips from the great Jewish comedians, most of whom got their start in New York.

At the **New-York Historical Society**, you'll see fascinating bits and pieces of Old New York, including 132 lamps by the city's Tiffany Studios. Also on view are a selection of poignant exhibits from the aftermath of 9/11, including a piece of one of the planes, masks and hats used by rescue workers, and candles used during vigils when the city came together. Few mementoes of that terrible day are sadder, or more important a part of the recent history of this great city.

Jewish Museum, Fifth Ave/92nd St; tel: 212-423-3200; www.thejewishmuseum. org; Sat–Wed 11am–5.45pm, Thur 11am–8pm, Fri 11am–4pm; map G5
New-York Historical Society, Central Park W. at 77th St; tel: 212-873-3400; www.nyhistory.org; Tue–Thur, Sat 10am–6pm, Fri to 8pm, Sun 11am–5.45pm; map D4

Pay homage at a **temple of gastronomy**

Time was, Central Park was the great divide when it came to food – one dined on the Upper East Side and simply ate on the Upper West Side. These days you can dine exquisitely on either side of the park and should make it a point to venture north of 59th Street, east or west, for at least one meal.

To say **Daniel** is one of the city's temples of gastronomy would sound more trite than it does if the opulent dining room weren't so beautifully graced with rows of Greek-looking columns and if chef Daniel Boulud weren't the high priest of innovative French cuisine, elevating such basics as ribs and pork belly to divine realms (closed on Sunday).

An old-fashioned, comfortingly dowdy Parisian elegance prevails at **Picholine**, where chef Terrance Brennan entrusts the excitement factor to the kitchen. As sea urchin panna cotta topped with caviar, polenta served with tuna bacon, and the finest selection of cheeses in New York roll out, the muted colors and subdued lighting become brighter by the moment.

Jean-Georges Vongerichten's restaurants cover the planet, and the epicenter of the empire is the airily stunning **Jean-Georges** overlooking Central Park. Creations such as wild mushroom tea and beef tenderloin topped with foie gras quickly put to rest any fears that expanding the brand has taken away from serious cooking. At just under $30 for two courses, Jean-Georges is the best weekday lunch deal in New York (reserve, closed Sunday).

Daniel, 60 E. 65th St; tel: 212-288-0033; http://danielnyc.com; map E1
Picholine, 35 W. 64th St; tel: 212-724-8585; www.picholinenyc.com; map C2
Jean-Georges, 1 Central Park West; tel: 212-299-3900; www.jean-georges.com; map C2

Go behind the gilded doorways of **Old New York** at the intimate **Frick Collection**

While it's often said that money does not buy good taste (step into Trump Tower in Midtown to see how true that is), steel magnate Henry Clay Frick had plenty of both. The serenely beautiful limestone mansion he built in 1914 is now the intimate Frick Collection, filled with works by Vermeer, Rembrandt, Ingres, Fragonard, and other European artists, each one a masterpiece.

The collection is relatively small. You can take a leisurely tour of the 16 galleries in less than an hour, with stops to linger in front of the pictures that capture your attention. One that certainly should is Francesco Guardi's *View of Venice*, full of vibrant light and dazzling water that will make you yearn for a setting as beautiful and exotic as the scene the artist captures. One is near at hand. Just down the corridor is an atrium filled with exotic palms and statuary surrounding a fountain and pool. The story goes that Frick said he created all this opulence to make business rival Andrew Carnegie's mansion at 92nd Street and Fifth Avenue, now the Cooper-Hewitt Museum, 'look like a miner's shack.' That would be hard to do, and both houses are rich remnants of New York in the Gilded Age.

Bemelman's Bar (Carlyle Hotel, 35 E. 76th St) just around the corner is the sort of dim, elegantly hushed place where glamorous characters in old movies set in New York engage in sophisticated banter, as have such real life regulars as Jackie O.

Frick Collection, Fifth Ave and 70th St; tel: 212-288-0700; www.frick.org; Tue–Sat 10am–6pm, Sun 11am–5pm; charge; map E2

Unwind with **river views** at Riverside Park or a **swim in an exotic pool**

Island that Manhattan is, some of the city's most refreshing retreats are on the miles of waterfront acreage. On the Upper West Side, **Riverside Park** follows the Hudson River for almost 4 miles. You can plant yourself on a shady lawn for a picnic, or find refreshment at the park's riverside cafes at 70th Street, next to a pier where outdoor films are screened on Wednesday evenings at 8pm; at 79th Street, above the Boat Basin; and at 105th Street. On the Upper East Side, a long pier is a breezy riverside perch at 107th Street, and **Eli's Vinegar Factory** (431 E. 91st St, tel: 212-987-0885, off map), supplies prepared meals for a picnic in Carl Shurz Park, on the river at 86th Street.

Manhattan's **YMCA** is a lovely red-brick Italianate-style tower on 63rd Street near Central Park West. Swimmers will be delighted to discover two large and stylish pools in the depths of the building, both surrounded by beautiful hand-decorated Italian tiles that create the exotic aura of a Roman nymphaeum (Mon–Fri 5am–10.45pm, Sat–Sun 8am–7.45pm, map C2). The longest pool in Manhattan, a full Olympic-length 50 meters, is at **Asphalt Green**, a large sports complex. Both have well-equipped gyms, as well as saunas and steam rooms. The best place for an outdoor dip is the **John Jay Pool** (June–early Sept, 11am–7pm, map H2) tucked into a patch of greenery next to the East River at the east end of 77th Street. Locker facilities are minimal (bring your own lock), but on a hot summer day all you'll really care about is diving into the refreshing water.

Enjoy a night at the **Opera**

Opera, it's said not entirely irreverently, is when a guy gets stabbed and instead of bleeding, he sings. This sentiment captures the magic of the wildly extravagant art form, and New York is blessed with one of the world's best opera companies. The Metropolitan Opera has staged dozens of American and world premieres, from Italian *bel canto* classics to new work, and presents the finest voices in the world. Enrico Caruso, Maria Callas, Luciano Pavarotti, Placido Domingo, Renée Fleming, and just about every other voice familiar even to non-opera buffs have sung on its enormous stage. The Met also pioneered innovative technology that allows simultaneous translation on computer screens in front of each of the 3,900 seats.

For all these superlatives, the Met is also remarkably proletarian – you can enjoy one of the majestic productions for as little as $35 for a seat in the family circle or even less with day-of-performance discounts. And you should – a night at the Met is right near the top of the list of only-in-New York experiences. Should you be mesmerized, you can go backstage to see such stage-magic wonders as a turntable 60 feet in diameter on tours during the season most weekdays at 3.30pm and Sundays at 10.30pm, for $15.

The Met's home is the **Lincoln Center for the Performing Arts**, a 16-acre campus on the Upper West Side the company shares with such illustrious neighbors as the New York Philharmonic, the New York City Ballet, and the City Opera. The season runs from October through May; the box office is in the foyer of the Metropolitan Opera House.

Metropolitan Opera House, Broadway at 64th St; tel: 212-362-6000; www. metopera.org; Mon–Sat 10am–8pm, Sun 10am–6pm; map B2
Day-of discount tickets are available from the David Rubenstein Atrium across the street on Broadway between West 62nd and West 63rd streets.

Catch some outdoor culture in **Central Park**

While Central Park is often touted as the greensward where New Yorkers escape their concrete canyons and get in touch with nature, what really makes these 837 acres so intriguing are the antics of New Yorkers. To paraphrase Shakespeare, all Central Park is a stage.

The park's official stage is the outdoor **Delacorte Theater** (map E4) where the New York Shakespeare Festive mounts two productions a summer. Meryl Streep, Anne Hathaway, Morgan Freeman, and Al Pacino are among the many stars who have performed in recent seasons against a sylvan backdrop of the Turtle Pond, a green sweep of grass and trees, and Belvedere Castle. Tickets are free, but you may consider getting one to be yet another challenge this hard-edged city throws at you or just part of the fun – that depends on how you feel about getting up at dawn and waiting in line for seven hours or so. Many inveterate theatergoers love the ritual, so join these bagel-munching know-it-alls to get an earful of inside dish on the New York theater world as you snake around the Great Lawn. Free tickets are distributed at 1pm on days of performances; for more info, go to www.publictheater.org.

No such hijinks are required to attend the summer performances by the Metropolitan Opera and New York Philharmonic. Thousands of listeners pour onto

PICNIC IN THE PARK

Below New York is the solid bedrock that provides a firm foundation for the city's iconic skyscrapers. Most conveniently, outcroppings of these rocky underpinnings poke through the greenery of Central Park to provide perfect perches for picnics. Especially choice spots are the diminutive mountain range of bedrock that rises just to the south of the Turtle Pond (the highest summit is crowned by Belvedere Castle) and a rocky landscape that rises and falls around the Carrousel, just east of the zoo. Another sylvan spot is the Pinaetum, a fragrant grove of pines at the northern edge of the Great Lawn. A convenient stop for provisions is **Whole Foods**, in the Time-Warner Center on Columbus Circle, at the southwestern end of the park.

the **Great Lawn** (map E4) to dine alfresco, listen to *bel canto* and symphonies, and safely enjoy the park under the night sky (even in post-gentrification New York, at other times it's still provident to keep in mind the advice of poet Ogden Nash, 'If you should happen after dark / To find yourself in Central Park / Ignore the paths that beckon you /And hurry, hurry to the zoo / And creep into the tiger's lair. Frankly you'll be safer there').

You're likely to come upon a performance or two at just about any time in the park, especially on weekends. **Bethesda Terrace** (map E3), where a lovely broad staircase descends to an ornate fountain and the lakeshore, is an impromptu stage for drummers, mimes, puppeteers, and other performers good enough to draw large, appreciative crowds of onlookers. The north end of Literary Walk, a stately promenade lined with elms and statues of poets, is the incongruous haunt of break dancers and rappers. **Strawberry Fields**, a beautifully planted oasis (map D3) near West 72nd Street that memorializes John Lennon, inspires many visitors to strum guitars and sing Beatles songs.

Central Park, map C1–G5
For information on concerts and other events, go to www.centralpark.com

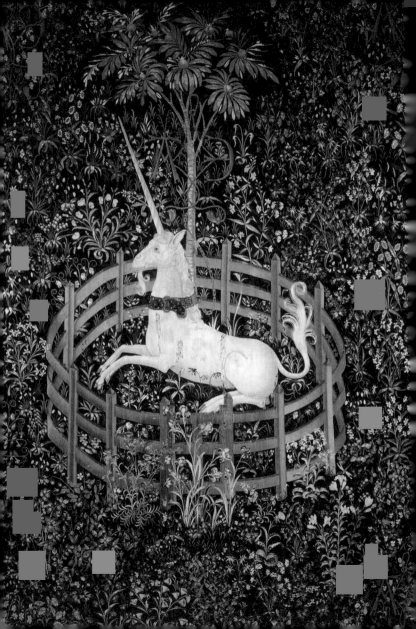

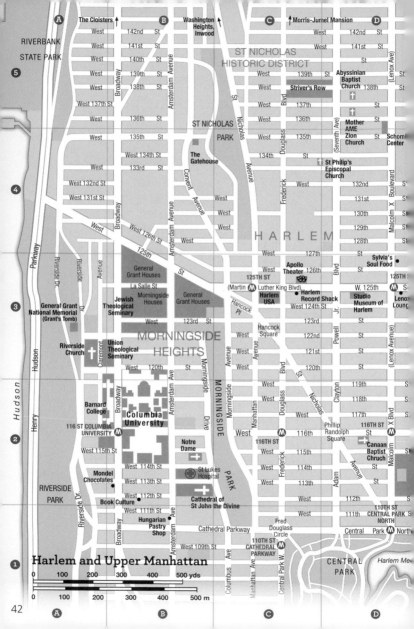

Harlem and Upper Manhattan

| 0 | 100 | 200 | 300 | 400 | 500 yds |
| 0 | 100 | 200 | 300 | 400 | 500 m |

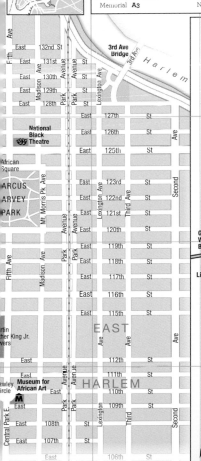

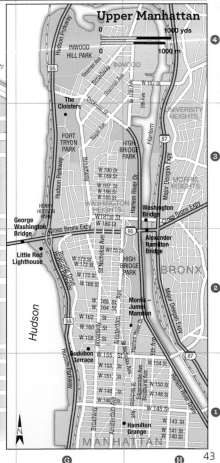

Upper Manhattan

Feel the vibe on **125th Street**, Harlem's main thoroughfare

The main thoroughfare of Harlem, legendary 125th Street, saw its heydays in the 1920s, '30s, and '40s, when Billie Holiday, Langston Hughes, James Baldwin, and other black cultural icons of the 20th century called the neighborhood home. Harlem and its famous avenue had fallen prey to urban woes by the 1970s and, depending on who's doing the talking, is now being restored to its former glory or is rapidly becoming just another string of chain stores. So, take a walk and judge for yourself; the 2, 3, A, B, C, or D subways will whisk you uptown to 125th Street. You'll soon be surrounded by a cluster of Starbucks, H&M, and Old Navy outlets around Fifth Avenue and St Nicholas Avenue that lend credence to the darker side of

the argument. But take heart: a welcome new neighbor is former president Bill Clinton, whose offices are in the Adam Clayton Powell Jr office building between Lenox and St Nicholas avenues.

Mr Clinton's choice of locale is one of the neighborhood's most heartening tales of recent years, as is the tenuous presence of the **Harlem Record Shack** (274 W. 125th St, map C3). The purveyor of jazz, Gospel, R&B, and hip-hop won an eviction battle a few years back, and owner Sikhulu Shange became the voice of local preservationists when he said, 'Tourists are not coming here to see McDonald's and Burger King. They are coming here to see black culture.' Other neighborhood institutions are the **Apollo Theater** (*see opposite*) and the **Lenox Lounge** (288 Lenox Ave, tel: 212-427-0253, map D3) where John Coltrane and Miles Davis were once regulars, and Patience Higgins, Hank Johnson, and current jazz greats still pack the house. A tribute to the ongoing spirit of the street is the **Studio Museum of Harlem** (144 W. 125th St, tel: 212-864-4500, Wed–Fri, Sun noon–6pm, Sat 10am–6pm, free on Sunday, map D3), showing the work of contemporary black artists from around the world.

Catch a rising star at the **Apollo Theater**

One night in the fall of 1934, a young woman stood backstage at the Apollo Theater, sweating and in obvious discomfort. A stage hand asked if she was ill. No, she replied, she wasn't ill. 'It's that audience, man. You never know what they're gonna do till you get out there.' The woman was Ella Fitzgerald, then just 17. The occasion was Amateur Night, the show 'where stars are born and legends are made' that also launched the careers of Billie Holiday, Michael Jackson, Sarah Vaughan, The Supremes, and many of the biggest names in 20th-century black entertainment.

As you will learn on a tour of the legendary theater, Ms Fitzgerald had good reason to be terrified. Audiences were notoriously vocal in their displeasure, and if less than pleased they would yell for the 'executioner,' a man with a broom who would sweep the contestant off stage. You'll also hear how, when the theater opened in 1914, blacks were not admitted. By the mid-1930s, the Apollo was featuring such all-black revues as Jazz a la Carte and 16 Gorgeous Hot Steppers and was at the center of the Harlem Renaissance, the great surge of music and literature that swept through New York's famous black neighborhood in the 1930s and '40s.

More than 75 years after the first legends got their start at Amateur Night, the show goes on – every Wednesday, at 7.30pm.

Apollo Theater box office: 253 West 125th St; tel: 212-531-5300; www. apollotheater.org; tours: Mon–Tue, Thur–Fri at 11am, 1pm, and 3pm, Wed at 11am, Sat–Sun at 11am and 1pm; map C3

Step into the Middle Ages at **the Cloisters** and explore its **peaceful wooded surroundings**

Modern Manhattan becomes magnificently medieval at the Cloisters, an outpost of the Metropolitan Museum of Art tucked away in the Fort Tryon Park at the far northern tip of the island. Five cloisters from southern France have been reassembled on a bluff high above the Hudson River, and they are surrounded by atmospheric galleries filled with 5,000 pieces of European art and architecture from the Middle Ages. Each vaulted room and stone-walled corridor reveals another treasure: as you meander you'll come upon seven wall hangings of the Unicorn Tapestry *(see picture p. 40)*, a 12th-century monastery chapter house, a Romanesque chapel, the sumptuously illustrated book of hours of the Duc de Berry, ivory crosses, carved portals, and a deck of 15th-century playing cards.

The greatest pleasure is seeking out a corner of one of the cloisters and quietly contemplating the surroundings. An especially peaceful spot is the 13th-century Bonnefont Cloister, from a Cistercian abbey and surrounded by simple columns that were left undecorated in case they should distract the monks from prayer. Beds are shaded by quince trees and planted with more than 400

herbs that surround a beautiful marble well, and the surroundings are not only serene but aromatic.

When industrialist and philanthropist John D. Rockefeller donated the Cloisters to the city in the 1930s, he threw hundreds of parkland acres across the Hudson River in the New Jersey Palisades into the deal. You will appreciate his foresight when you step out onto the West Terrace and take in the generous sweep of river and greenery, so unspoiled that the medieval surroundings seem remarkably in place.

FORT TRYON PARK

The Cloisters is nestled within densely wooded Fort Tryon Park, on high ground that once harbored Weckquaesgeek Indians, Dutch colonialists, and the Continental Army, who established a series of outposts on bluffs they collectively called Fort Washington. More than 8 miles of paths traverse the woods and come to terraces overlooking the Hudson River. As you explore this beautiful and uncrowded park, stop in at the **New Leaf Restaurant and Bar** (L and D Tue–Sun, tel: 212-568-5323) in a stone building at the park entrance, with a lovely patio.

The Cloisters, Fort Tryon Park; tel: 212-923-3700; www.metmuseum.org; Tue–Sun 9am–5.15pm; suggested donation $20; map G3

47

Visit the **Little Red Lighthouse** and take a bracing walk across the **George Washington Bridge**

Manhattan's mighty towers often soar above much humbler structures, creating some of the city's many visual treats. Nowhere is this juxtaposition more endearing than on the banks of the Hudson River at 178th Street, where the **Little Red Lighthouse** stands modestly but proudly in the shadows of the steel girders and concrete abutments of the George Washington Bridge. Both structures are beloved New York landmarks, though the lighthouse that once guided boat traffic up and down the river has not flashed its beacon since the bridge was completed in 1931. You can tour the lighthouse on some weekends from spring through fall, and any youngster who has read *The Little Red Lighthouse and the Great Gray Bridge* will want to do so. In the 1942 classic the lighthouse

becomes convinced it is no longer needed when a beacon begins flashing atop the bridge, but comes to the rescue one foggy night to warn boats away from the rocks, proving that the big and the small are both important.

You can walk to New Jersey and back across the 600-foot-high, 4,750-foot-long **George Washington Bridge** on a walkway elevated more than 200 feet above the river. The trek is especially rewarding on a clear day, when you can see south to the city skyline and way upriver to the forested hills that cradle the Hudson Valley. You can enter the walkway from Fort Washington Avenue and 178th Street. To reach the lighthouse, follow the well-marked path from Lafayette Street and 181st Street.

Information tel: 212-304-2365; map G2

Step back in time to the **grand old homes** of **early New Yorkers**

Two old homes, hidden among 20th-century apartment blocks, are especially evocative of the first days of the fledging nation, and they honor some pretty colorful early New Yorkers, too.

At the **Morris-Jumel Mansion**, *(pictured)* it's easy to imagine beautiful Eliza Jumel gliding across the creaking pine floors and settling into one of the French Empire silk chairs. Eliza was no stuffy colonial dame. A former prostitute, she worked her way into 'proper' society and married wealthy wine merchant Stephen Jumel. In 1810 the couple bought a Palladian-style house that was built in 1765, became the Revolutionary War headquarters of George Washington, and is now the oldest home in Manhattan. Before long Eliza was a wealthy widow and advanced her status even further by marrying vice president Aaron Burr – from whom she soon filed for divorce, when she discovered how quickly her new husband was going through her fortune.

Among Eliza's neighbors were the wife and children of Alexander Hamilton, first US secretary of the treasury, who in 1802 built a manor house, **the Grange**, on 32 acres of orchards, gardens, and parkland. The house shows off fine early American furniture, but the private life of Hamilton was a lot less tidy. His affair with a married woman, Maria Reynolds, was one of the great scandals of early American politics, and in 1804 he was shot dead – by none other than Aaron Burr. The Grange has since been moved to St Nicholas Park, and the greenery outside the windows suggests the open land that once surrounded the house. The Morris-Jumel Mansion is at the end of **Sylvan Terrace**, a lane of wooden row houses from the 1880s.

Morris-Jumel Mansion, 65 Jumel Terrace (off 160th St); tel: 212-923-8008; www.morrisjumel.org; Wed–Sun 10am–4pm; charge; map H2
Hamilton Grange, St Nicholas Park, 141st St and Convent Ave; tel: 212-666-1640; www.nps.gov/hagr; call or check online for hours; free; map H1

Hear **Gospel music** and enjoy **soul food** in Harlem

Two fine old institutions, one appealing to the soul, the other to the stomach, will introduce you to the spirit of Harlem. You can experience them in half a day – provided the day is a Sunday, and you are willing to make an early start to attend one of the Gospel services at 9 or 11am at the **Abyssinian Baptist Church** (*pictured*). Ethiopian seamen founded the congregation in lower Manhattan in 1818 (choosing the ancient name of their homeland). Reverend Adam Clayton Powell Sr moved the church to its beautiful neo-Gothic home in 1923; his son, Adam Clayton Powell Jr, became the first black congressman in US history. Abyssinian is still a vigorous voice for social justice, and the church also puts on one heck of a show when the beautiful sounds of the choir ring out in a sanctuary lit by a sea of stained glass. Visitors are asked to wait for admittance in a special queue and to dress appropriately – that means arriving early and wearing your Sunday best if you expect to fit in with the congregation.

Sylvia's Soul Food (328 Lenox Avenue, tel: 212-996-0660), several blocks south, serves a post-service brunch of such stick-to-your ribs basics as fried chicken and sweet potato pie. Sylvia's has been a Harlem institution since it opened the restaurant in 1962, and is still run by Sylvia Woods, the 'Queen of Soulfood,' and her children and grandchildren.

You'll need to walk off that meal, so head back up Adam Clayton Powell Jr Boulevard to 138th and 139th streets, collectively known as **Strivers' Row**. Some of New York's most beautiful blocks were built for wealthy whites in the 1890s but, as the neighborhood became black, were sold off to black middle-class professionals known as 'strivers.' Today, Strivers' Row is prime real estate, and you will easily see why.

Abyssinian Baptist Church, 132 Odell Clark Place; tel: 212-862-7474; map D5

Come face to face with a gargoyle at the colossal
Cathedral of St John the Divine

The Cathedral of St John the Divine is usually described in superlatives that refer to the church's enormous size – St John's is the fourth-largest Christian church and largest Gothic cathedral in the world, and the rose window, best appreciated from Broadway and 112th Street, is the largest stained-glass window in the United States, containing more than 10,000 colored pieces. You'll get a sense of the sheer vastness of the place – two football fields long and 17 stories tall – as soon as you step inside.

Like the rest of ever-changing Manhattan, the cathedral is a perpetual construction site, and has been a work in progress since 1892. Unlike many of the great European cathedrals, set off in greenery, St John is squeezed onto its urban site, giving the impression that the church is even bigger than it is. Provided you don't succumb to vertigo, you can get a good perspective of the overwhelming vastness of the church on a Vertical Tour. You will climb high above the nave on spiral staircases, cross the flying buttresses, and emerge next to the gargoyles on the roof, peering at carvings and stained glass as you go.

Cathedral of St John the Divine, 112th St and Amsterdam Ave. Vertical Tour: Sat only, noon and 2pm, charge; other tours are conducted throughout the week; For more information, call 212-932-7347; map B2

Explore a **college town** in the city

New York does not even come close to anyone's notion of a typical college town, but the streets around Columbia have a faint whiff of collegiality to them – fueled by 26,000 students as well the many artistically inclined, rather bohemian New Yorkers who call this part of the Upper West Side home. Follow them to their lairs, and you will find some especially quirky corners of New York.

The neighborhood's favorite gathering spot is the **Hungarian Pastry Shop**, a cramped, funky, utterly charming room across the street from the Cathedral of St John the Divine. The delicious, buttery pastries pre-date our obsession with caloric intake, coffee refills are free, and,

eavesdropping from the packed-together tables, you'll get an earful of vicarious gossip about the lives and loves of young and restless students and also be privy to heated debates over the war in Iraq and other weighty affairs.

Book Culture, around the corner, has all the friendly hallmarks of a hometown bookstore – that is, if you hail from a fairly intellectually inclined town. You'll have better luck finding a new release on European aesthetics than you will the latest page-turner by Danielle Steel. The well-displayed selections from small and university presses provide an insightful brush with the current intellectual front.

The neighborhood indulges in non-cerebral satisfaction at **Mondel Chocolates**, whose legendary house-made confections such as Turtles, breakups, and mint squares, were described by Katharine Hepburn as the 'best in the world.' The late actress sent her driver uptown for a weekly supply of its delicious offerings.

Hungarian Pastry Shop, 1030 Amsterdam Ave at 111th St; tel: 212-866-4230; map B1
Book Culture, 536 W. 112th St; tel: 212-865-1588; map B2
Mondel Chocolates, 2913 Broadway; tel: 212-864-2111; map B2

Step through the gates and into the grand Beaux-Arts campus of **Columbia University**

ALMA MATER

Students at Columbia University follow in the footsteps of eminent alumni who include four US presidents, and 93 Nobel Prize winners. The campus of this distinguished institution, founded in 1754, is fittingly monumental, one of the most impressive public spaces in New York and the city's homage to neoclassical style.

You can get a good look at Columbia just by wandering through the Main Gate, at 116th Street and Broadway, into the quadrangle. Several cupolas, including the largest granite dome in America, rise above the orderly progression of facades. Low Library is modeled after Rome's Pantheon. The broad granite Low staircase sweeps up from the quad to an upper terrace and bronze doors that open to a grand rotunda. About halfway up the steps is the *Alma Mater*. Pause in front of the seated figure to take in the sweep of red brick and green grass. Then look into the folds of her cloak, where, with a bit of searching, you will discover a small owl – a symbol that knowledge can be hard to find and as touching a tribute to this great university's intellectual pursuits as the grand monuments surrounding you.

Columbia University; free tours Mon–Fri, from the Visitor's Center, Low Library; tel: 212-854-4900; map B2

53

Enjoy a **carillon concert** and a pretty patch of greenery at **Sakura Park**

Should you find yourself on Riverside Drive at 121st Street on Sundays at 10.30am, 12.30pm, or 3pm, you will be treated to a free concert – a very loud concert provided by 74 bronze bells, including a 20-ton monster that is the heaviest bell ever cast, presented to **Riverside Church** by John D. Rockefeller in memory of his mother. The bells are installed in a carillon that rises 392 feet above the city, gracing New York with a skyscraper bell tower that is, quite fittingly, the world's tallest. Martin Luther King Jr, Nelson Mandela, and other world figures have spoken beneath the church's acres of stained glass.

Sakura Park, at the base of the tower, is one of the prettiest patches of greenery in New York, and with its tidy gravel paths and orderly rows of trees, seems like an elegant square in Paris. In fact, a soft gray Parisian melancholy washes over this quiet stretch of Riverside Drive, providing suitable surroundings for Grant's Tomb, the somber mausoleum of the Civil War general and 18th president of the United States, Ulysses S. Grant.

Just up the street is a more humble, yet touching memorial 'to the memory of an amiable child ... 5-year-old who fell to his death from these rocks on July 15, 1797.'

The schist that begins to emerge in the neighborhood becomes more pronounced the farther north you go. By 181st Street, the island's rocky underpinnings erupt in a tall cliff that was a strategic stronghold during the Revolutionary War, when patriots lost the Battle of Fort Washington from ramparts that are now outlined in granite blocks.

Riverside Church, 490 Riverside Drive at 121st St; tel: 212-870-6700; map A3

Rub shoulders with Spanish Old Masters on
Audubon Terrace

Step west off Broadway at 155th Street, climb the short flight of steps, walk through the tall iron gates, and you'll be transported to one of the most elegant yet little-known corners of New York, Audubon Terrace. The assemblage of colonnaded Beaux-Arts limestone facades rising above a handsome brick walk was erected in the early 20th century by railroad heir Archer Milton Huntington on the former estate of John James Audubon, the famous American wildlife artist.

The Terrace is home to the **Hispanic Society of America**. Beyond the proud portals of this august institution you will be transported even further, into a dark Spanish palace hung with works by El Greco, Velázquez, and a Goya masterpiece, the portrait of his mistress, the *Duchess of Alba*. The high-ceilinged galleries surround an inner court modeled after the courtyard of a castle in Spain. Audubon Terrace exudes an air of faded glory and forgotten grandeur, making the place all the more charming, and one of the city's most welcome retreats.

Audubon Terrace, 613 W. 155th St; tel: 212-926-2234; Tue–Sat 10am–4.30pm, Sun 1am–4pm; free; map G2

A SCULPTURE GARDEN
Another peace-inducing New York oasis is the **Noguchi Museum** (32–37 Vernon Blvd, Long Island City, tel: 718-204-7088, www.noguchi.org, Wed–Fri 10am–5pm, Sat–Sun 11am–6pm) in Queens. A former gas station and photogravure plant have been fashioned into a museum-garden to house the stone, steel, wood, and paper works of Japanese-American sculptor and designer Isamu Noguchi (1904–88). The serene surroundings are an island of calm in the industrial neighborhood, all the better to show off the beautiful mastery of Noguchi, whose works grace urban spaces around the world. His **Red Cube** is a colorful landmark in the Financial District, at 140 Broadway.

55

Midtown

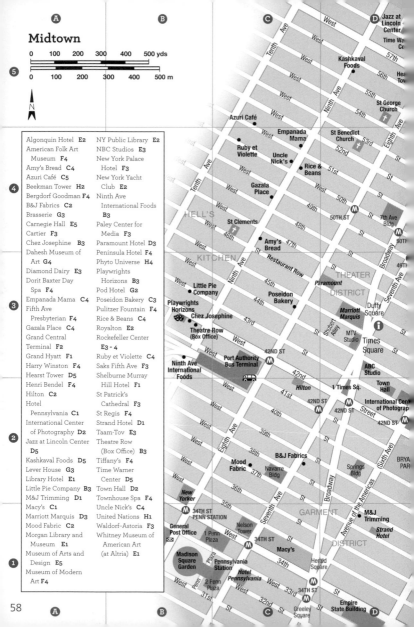

Midtown

Drink in the lights from a **hideaway in the sky**

While some of the city's famous old-time hideaways in the sky have gone the way of the subway token – the Rainbow Room is locked up tight and Top of the Sixes is a private cigar club for big shots – you can linger over a drink with city lights twinkling at your toes in plenty of other aeries.

Four Midtown hotel rooftops are especially appealing retreats from the city streets below, and all afford views that are as intoxicating as the cocktails. Top marks for sophistication go to **Salon de Ning** *(pictured)* atop the Peninsula Hotel (700 Fifth Ave at 55th St, tel: 212-956-2888, map F4). The Asian-infused decor evoking the feel of 1930s Shanghai is glamorous, and the light show of the surrounding Midtown towers even more so. So much Art Deco élan pervades the 1920s-era **Top of the Tower** (Beekman Tower Hotel, 49th St and First Ave, tel: 212- 355-7300, map H2) that you'll be inspired to engage in some wittily urbane Noel Coward-style banter, and the 360-degree views take in the Midtown skyline, the East River, and a large swath of Queens that, all aglow once the sun sets, looks much more wondrous than it really is. Greenery and sophistication are profuse at the **Top of the Strand** (Strand Hotel, 33 W. 37th St, tel: 212-448-1024, map D1), and the Empire State Building is so close you'll be tempted to reach out and touch it. **Rare**, on the 16th floor of the Shelburne Murray Hill (303 Lexington Ave at 37th St, tel: 212-481-8439, map F1) is also dramatically over-shadowed by the Empire State Building, while the Chrysler Building spire appears as a shiny beacon just to the north.

Go behind the scenes of hit TV shows at NBC

At 49th Street, Fifth Avenue lives up to its lofty reputation with the **Rockefeller Center**, one of the world's biggest business and entertainment complexes, and a triumph of Art Deco architecture. Rockefeller Plaza is dominated by the 70 floors of the soaring GE Building, number 30 Rockefeller Center, or '30 Rock' – headquarters of NBC. Anyone can be part of a live audience any weekday morning during NBC's long-running *Today Show*, which is broadcast from a glassed-in studio on the corner of 49th Street, but to get a good spot you should arrive about 6am.

COMEDY CENTRAL
If you're a fan of political comedy, you can join the studio audience of a weekday taping of Jon Stewart's satirical news show *The Daily Show* or Stephen Colbert's equally irreverent *The Colbert Report*. Both Emmy Award-winning presenters have won huge popularity in the US and abroad for their deadpan mockery of political punditry.

You need to book tickets well in advance, then be prepared to line up – rain or shine – for 2-3 hours outside **Comedy Central Studios** (11th Ave and 52nd St, off map) for the tapings that end about 7pm. Order the tickets online at www.thedailyshow.com/tickets.com or www.colbertnation/tickets.com.

If you want to see where hit shows like *Saturday Night Live*, *NBC Nightly News* or *Late Night with Jimmy Fallon* are made, sign up for the **NBC Studio tour** at the NBC Experience Store. These behind-the-scenes tours depart every 15 minutes and give you a chance to see the corridors and rooms that influenced the hit show *30 Rock*. Each tour lasts about 70 minutes and takes you into a control studio, make-up room, and several show studios.

NBC Experience Store, 30 Rockefeller Plaza, 49th St between Fifth and Sixth aves; tours Mon–Thur 8.30am–5.30pm, Fri–Sat until 6.30pm, Sun until 4.30pm. For tickets, tel: 212-664-3700 or book in advance at www.nbcuniversalstore.com; map E3

Take a **stroll through classic New York**, then head to the **Top of the Rock** to view it all from above

Much of Midtown evokes the 1930s, a decade that, to paraphrase Charles Dickens, 'was the best of times and the worst of times' for New York. Though reeling from the Great Depression, the city was gripped by a building spree. A forest of new skyscrapers, mighty symbols of American enterprise, began to soar above Midtown.

The 14 Art Deco towers of the **Rockefeller Center**, between 48th and 51st streets off Fifth Avenue (map E4), constitute a city within the city. Walk down the **Channel Gardens**, a beautiful promenade that separates the French Building from the British Building, and raise your eyes along the 70-story height of 30 Rockefeller Plaza. You can't help but feel as though you are gazing up at a great temple of commerce. Meanwhile, the spires of **St Patrick's Cathedral** across

Fifth Avenue (map F3) seem to lift you from the pavement toward heavenly heights.

Over on Park Avenue are two monuments to another hope-filled age, the 1950s. **Lever House**, at 390 Park Avenue (map G3), and the **Seagram Building**, across the street at 375 Park (map G3), are sleek steel-and-glass towers that rise from airy plazas. Together they secured a place for the functional glass office tower on the American landscape. They have inspired hundreds of imitators, none of which are as beautiful or as suggestive of corporate might as these two Park Avenue neighbors.

Art and Observation tours of the Rockefeller Center show off murals, statues, and architectural highlights, and end on the observation platform of **Top of the Rock**, an exhilarating open-air

viewpoint (*pictured*) 70 floors above the city (90 mins, www.nbcuniversalstore.com, Mon–Sat 10am–2pm, map E4)

A PAIR OF BEAUTIES

The **Empire State Building**, at 34th Street and Fifth Avenue (map D1), long ago ceded the world's tallest title, but the beloved granite tower is still New York's most popular skyscraper. A very close second place goes to the **Chrysler Building** (map F1), with a shiny stainless steel crown that evokes the wonders of the machine age and rises high above Lexington Avenue and 42nd Street. Their presence on the skyline is testimony to a longstanding rivalry. The Chrysler Building was the tallest structure in the world, the first ever to surpass 1,000 feet, when it was completed in 1929 – the spire, which was secretly assembled within the upper floors then hoisted into position, jostled a newly completed tower at 40 Wall Street out of first-place position. Just two years later the Empire State Building surpassed its neighbor by 250 feet. Though skyscrapers pierce the clouds above cities around the world, none can match the appeal of this pair of Art Deco beauties.

The 86th-floor observation deck of the Empire State Building (daily 8am–2am) treats 3.5 million visitors a year to eagle's-eye views; among the standouts is the nearby Chrysler Building, whose gargoyles fashioned in the shape of radiator caps and hood ornaments shine brightly on a sunny day.

Admire a modern masterpiece at **MoMA** or a rare manuscript at the **Morgan Library**

The **Museum of Modern Art** houses a collection of 150,000 paintings, sculptures, photographs, and other works, displayed in crisp contemporary galleries on West 53rd Street. MoMA is not as daring a design statement as such other showcases of modern art as the Tate Modern, the Pompidou Centre, or the Guggenheim Bilbao. Even so, as the vanguard of commerce and corporate might, Midtown provides an appropriate backdrop for the art movements that have broken new ground. Stepping off the busy Midtown avenues to stand in front of Picasso's *Les Demoiselles d'Avignon* or Rousseau's *The Sleeping Gypsy* is one of the city's most transporting experiences.

While MoMA celebrates the modern, the **Morgan Library and Museum** preserves some of the earliest examples of the written word. J. Pierpont Morgan, the great financier and banker, was a connoisseur of fine art and an avid collector of illuminated manuscripts, rare books, prints, and drawings. He left his entire collection to the city of New York. Galleries show off drawings by Michelangelo and Rembrandt, Gutenberg bibles, sheet music by Beethoven, and scraps of paper on which Bob Dylan jotted down lyrics for *Blowin' in the Wind*.

MoMA, West 53rd St; tel: 212-708-9400; www.moma.org; Sat-Tue 10.30am–5.30pm, Thur 10.30am–5.30pm (until 8.45pm in July and Aug), Fri 10.30am–8pm, free on Fri evenings; map F4
The Morgan Library and Museum, 225 Madison Ave; tel: 212-685-0008; www.themorgan.org; Tue–Thur 10.30am–5pm, Fri 10.30–9pm, Sat 10am–6pm, Sun 11am–6pm, free on Fri evenings; map E1

Have **breakfast near Tiffany's** and **shop** like a star in Fifth Avenue's most glittering stores

'Tiffany's! Cartier! Talk to me Harry Winston.' So Marilyn Monroe coos in her song *Diamonds Are a Girl's Best Friend*, seductively capturing the allure of shopping on Fifth Avenue around 57th Street. The glittering display windows of all three renowned jewelers, as well as some of the world's other finest shops, grace this stretch of the avenue.

Cartier (at 52nd St and Fifth Ave, map F3) has been bejeweling royalty since 1847, and along the way has made such savvy business maneuvers as introducing the first men's wristwatch, in 1904. The New York store occupies a beautiful mansion purchased in 1917 for $100 and a pearl necklace valued at $1 million.

The **Harry Winston** (at 56th St and Fifth Ave, map F4) collection once included the deep-blue 45.52 carat Hope Diamond (now in the Smithsonian Institution in Washington DC). The shop still sells distinctive jewels in service to the founder's informal motto, 'People will stare. Make it worth their while.'

Tiffany's (at 57th St and Fifth Ave, map F4) was founded in 1834, and moved to its distinctive limestone flagship store in 1940. Over the years the vendor of

jewelry, silverware, and stationery has catered to Astors, Vanderbilts, Rockefellers, and others for whom the Tiffany name is the epitome of refinement.

While it is not possible to have breakfast at Tiffany's, a coffee and croissant in the nearby **Brasserie**, (100 E. 53rd St, tel: 212-751-4840, Mon–Fri from 7am, Sat–Sun from 11am, map G3) will start off a morning of shopping in suitably stylish fashion.

A trilogy of nearby Fifth Avenue department stores, **Saks** (at 50th St, map F3), **Henri Bendel** (at 57th St, map F4) and **Bergdorf Goodman** (at 57th St, map F4) are venues for a slightly more affordable, but no less refined shopping spree.

Be transported by **Grand Central Terminal**

One of the architectural gems of New York City, Grand Central Terminal is worth spending time in even if you aren't going anywhere. Completed in 1913 after nearly a decade of construction, the beautiful Beaux-Arts station ushered in the era of electric train travel. Many of the grand apartment buildings and hotels in the area were erected around the new terminal, including The Roosevelt Hotel, The Park Lane, and The Waldorf-Astoria. By 1947, Grand Central Terminal was one of the most important transportation hubs in North America. That year more than 65 million people passed through, equal to about 40% of the US population of the time. But car travel and suburban living in the 1950s drastically reduced station traffic, and the building fell into disrepair. By the mid-1960s the roof was leaking and soot and grime covered the walls. Wrecking crews stood by while a protracted battle between conservationists, led by Jackie Onassis, and developers raged on. The station was finally saved by a Supreme Court ruling in 1978, and in the 1990s, a $425 million renovation project restored it to its original magnificence. Today Grand Central Terminal is once again a valued central hub of the city thanks to an efficient commuter train service, a steady stream of tourists, dozens of high-end shops, five restaurants , a cocktail lounge, and more than 20 eateries on the lower level.

ARCHITECTURAL HIGHLIGHTS

The magnificent illuminated zodiac on the vaulted ceiling, painted in gold leaf on cerulean blue oil, now gleams like new. All apart, that is, from a dark patch on the northwest lower corner. This was left untouched to give an understanding of the extent of the restoration effort. The gold- and silver-plated chandeliers were designed to show off the cutting-edge technology of the early 1900s: the light bulb. A marble staircase was added to east end of the concourse, matching that of the west end (both modeled on the staircase of the Paris Opera) and the marble flooring is sprung like a dance floor – which explains the strangely muted sounds of travelers threading their way across the vast concourse. Free architectural tours are given every Wednesday at 12.30pm (meet at the central information booth).

Downstairs, outside the wonderful **Oyster Bar & Restaurant** (an architectural and culinary landmark), is the **Whispering Gallery**: two people standing in opposite corners of the archway can speak to each other while facing the wall. Try it! For a quick snack, choose from any of the quality eateries.

Return to ground level for a cocktail at the grand **Campbell Apartment** by the southeast entrance near Park Avenue, formerly the private office of Jazz Age business magnate John W. Campbell, now one of the most elegant bars in New York.

Round off your visit with some shopping at the station's high-end boutiques, or check out the temporary craft exhibits in **Vanderbilt Hall** near the 42nd Street main entrance.

Grand Central Terminal, at 42nd St between Park and Lexington aves; map F2

Immerse yourself in an elegant **Beaux-Arts library**, then relax in a pleasant **Midtown oasis**

On the west side of Fifth Avenue between 42nd and 40th streets you'll pass a monumental staircase flanked by two marble lions, *Patience* and *Fortitude*. They are the unofficial greeters to the **New York Public Library** and were named by Mayor Fiorello LaGuardia back in the 1930s for the qualities he wished New Yorkers to demonstrate. The city seems to have collectively rejected the first and embraced the other.

The lions are both proud and welcoming, as befits one of the world's great knowledge institutions, and they beckon passersby to come in and wander through marble hallways and handsome exhibition galleries to admire rare volumes, maps, prints, and photographs from the vast collections. The Rose Main Reading Room is furnished with 42 long oak tables and comfortable chairs, and warmly lit by tall windows, glowing chandeliers, and brass reading lamps. If you fill out a call slip, one of the library's 10 million volumes will be delivered to your seat from the 128 miles of shelves that wrap through the cellars and beneath adjacent Bryant Park. It's also nice just to sit back and take in the surroundings, appreciating the fact that a great city like New York has a fine library like this in its midst.

Bryant Park, behind the library, is one of New York's smaller but most appreciated public arenas. Throughout the year, a jaunty carrousel revolves to the sound of French cabaret music. In the winter, skaters glide across a skating rink; in the summer, office workers splay themselves on the lawns to steal a few moments in the sun, and filmgoers gather in the evenings to lie back and enjoy outdoor screenings.

New York Public Library, Fifth Ave at 42nd St; tel: 917-275-6975; www.nypl.org; Mon, Thur-Sat 10am-6pm, Tue-Wed 10am-9pm, closed Sun; free 1-hour tours Mon-Sat at 11 am and 2 pm; map E2

Sip a cocktail in style

With its concrete canyons and urbanity, Midtown is a place where you can easily imagine momentous events transpiring, big deals brokered, wise words uttered. The neighborhood is home to several venues that are especially well suited to such weighty affairs.

The **Algonquin Lounge** is a cushy lair in one of the city's best-loved old hotels. Ninety years ago it was the favorite lunch spot of a group of actors, writers and critics known as the Round Table. Talk could be vicious, but was unfailingly clever. During one of the lunches wisecracking satirist Dorothy Parker was asked to use the word 'horticulture' in a sentence and she replied, 'You can lead a horticulture but you can't make her think.'

The **King Cole Bar** off the lobby of the St Regis Hotel is a dark, woody hideaway that is wonderfully impervious to the march of time. Dress well, order a Bloody Mary (allegedly invented here), and ask the bartender to tell you what's really going on in the Maxfield Parrish mural of *Old King Cole* behind the bar *(pictured)*.

The Four Seasons has been the epitome of grown-up urbanity ever since it opened in the Seagram Building in 1959. Undulating walls of metal chain curtains envelop the space in a time warp, and the effect is magical. Philip Johnson, the legendary architect, designed the Four Seasons, and few of his many masterpieces are as beloved.

Algonquin Lounge, 59 W. 44th St; tel: 212-840-6800; map E2
King Cole Bar, 2 E. 55th St; tel: 212-753-4500, map F4
The Four Seasons, 99 E. 52nd St; tel: 212-754-9494; closed Sun; map G3

Give your regards to **Off-Broadway**

Once you've heard the beat of dancing feet on 42nd Street, keep heading west – to a block so chockablock with stages it's known as **Theatre Row**.

Time was, no one with reputable intentions would venture too far west in sleazy Times Square beyond the brightly lit arcades of the big Broadway theaters. These days, though, some of the city's most exciting

FARTHER OFF-BROADWAY

Two other Off-Broadway venues, a little further afield, also ensure a good night at the theater. *Hair, A Chorus Line*, and some of the other most exciting plays of the past 45 years have emerged from the **Public Theater** (425 Lafayette St, tel: 212-260-2400, www. publictheater.org, map p.132 B4) on Astor Place at the edge of the East Village. The Public is especially known for avant-garde drama and Shakespearian productions, staged in the outdoor **Delacorte Theater** in Central Park every summer *(see p.38)*. A Renaissance-style landmark that the Astor family, founders of the fur-trading empire, built in 1854 houses the Public's five year-round stages and Joe's Pub, a cabaret.

Les Mis and other blockbusters may pack Broadway houses to the rafters, but New York also nurtures excellent work that, as the old theater expression goes, will never play in Omaha. Modern and classic texts are given innovative interpretations by the **Wooster Group** (33 Wooster St, tel: 212-966-9796, www.thewoostergroup. org; map p.116 D3) at the Performing Garage, where productions often incorporate experimental uses of sound and video. **La MaMa** (74A E. 4th St, tel: 212-475-7710, www.lamama.org; map p.132 C4) has been presenting original performance pieces from around the world for almost 50 years, establishing itself as the beachhead of experimental theaters and a major force in presenting works by new playwrights.

WAY OFF-BROADWAY

The **Brooklyn Academy of Music** (451 Fulton St and other nearby venues, Brooklyn, tel: 718-636-7100, www.bam.org, map p.151, H3) was founded in 1861, making it America's oldest continually running performing arts center, and over the years has welcomed such legends as Enrico Caruso. These days, BAM is best known for its innovative productions, and, as if to demonstrate just how avant-garde BAM is, many are mounted in a former vaudeville house that has been dramatically deconstructed down to brick walls, peeling paint, and exposed masonry.

drama is staged on what was until recently an especially seedy strip of 42nd Street between Ninth and Tenth avenues. Former sex clubs and massage parlors are now home to almost a dozen Off-Broadway theaters such as the **Acorn** and the **Beckett**. (Off-Broadway is a term invented – to confuse just about anyone – it refers to theaters that seat between 99 and 500 patrons and has nothing to do with geographic location, though most Off-Broadway stages happen to be outside the theater district we think of as Broadway.) Several theaters on Theatre Row mount the

productions of **Playwrights Horizons**, committed to the work of contemporary American playwrights. The block also has a suitably dramatic restaurant, the legendary **Chez Josephine**, where Jean-Claude Baker recreates the 1930s Paris of his adoptive mother, Josephine Baker.

Theatre Row, box office, 410 W. 42nd St; tel: 212-714-2442; www.theatrerow.org; map B3
Playwrights Horizons, 416 W. 42nd St; tel: 212-564-1235; www.playwrightshorizons.org; map B3
Chez Josephine; 414 W. 42nd St; tel: 212-594-1925; Tue–Sat noon–1am, Sun noon–10pm; map B3

Pamper yourself at a **sumptuous spa**

What better way to take a break from the hard work of tourism than with a relaxing massage, a facial or a sauna at a high-end Midtown spa (but be prepared to splash out).

Enter the ornate and old-world glamour of the lobby of **The New York Palace Hotel**, then head to the spacious spa and fitness center on the eighth floor. Work out on a treadmill overlooking St Patrick's cathedral, have a sauna or steam bath, and enjoy a hot compress massage or back treatment.

Located in a townhouse renovated with a high-end Asian feel, **The Townhouse Spa** has a cozy women's area in the lower level, a restaurant and nail spa at street level, and a clubby atmosphere for men on the second floor. Enjoy a Shiatsu, Swedish and Stone therapy massage or the signature Townhouse Glow facial.

Phyto Universe is a spa for your hair in a balmy, lush oasis brought to you by the respected French hair product company. Experts in lab coats analyze strands of your hair and get a microscopic look at your scalp, then decide what treatments and products might be best for you.

If your wallet is hurting but you're looking for a high-quality spa experience, try the **Dorit**

Baxter Day Spa near Carnegie Hall, popular with actors and journalists. Ignore the sparse lobby and head upstairs and enjoy relaxing European facials, blissful Dead Sea salt scrubs, and massages using bamboo sticks.

New York Palace Hotel Spa, 455 Madison Ave; tel: 212-303-7777; www. newyorkpalace.com/spa-fitness; map F3
The Townhouse Spa, 39 W. 56th St; tel: 212-245-8006; www.townhousespa.com; map F4
Phyto Universe, 715 Lexington Ave; tel: 212-308-0270; www.phytouniverse.com; map H4
Dorit Baxter Day Spa, 47 W. 57th St # 301; tel: 212-371-4542; map F4

Be dazzled by glittering jewels in the
Diamond District

Even if you're not shopping for a diamond engagement ring, gold wedding band, or gemstone, a foray into the Diamond District on West 47th Street reveals a fascinating side of New York commerce. And if you are in the market for high-quality, well-priced jewelry, you've come to the right place. More than 2,500 independent businesses operate in the district, in street-level shops filled with glittering jewels, cellar workshops, and a glossy new skyscraper, the International Gem Tower. Many of the shops have been doing business since the 1930s and 40s, when Orthodox Jews fled the Nazi invasion of such European diamond centers as Antwerp and Amsterdam.

Shops are generally open Mon–Fri 9am–5pm. Very few will take checks, and many offer better deals if you pay cash. You may well feel a bit out of your depth entering the warren of dealers, so do a little online preparation before you hit the pavement. The Jewelers Vigilance Committee, www.jvclegal.org, provides a useful checklist of what to look for when buying fine jewelry, and the Gemological Institute of America, www.gia.edu, offers an online tutorial in diamond-buying.

Synagogues and restaurants are tucked away above shops and arcades. **Taam-Tov** (41) specializes in such Central Asian dishes as golubsy, cabbage leaves stuffed with rice and meat, while the **Diamond Dairy Kosher Luncheonette** (4) serves the best cheese blintzes in the city.

Diamond District, W. 47th St, between Fifth and Sixth aves; map E3

Be a **culture** vulture on **Columbus Circle**

Columbus Circle, the busy intersection of Broadway, Central Park West, Eighth Avenue, and Central Park South, is a whirl of traffic enlivened with fountains and statues and is surrounded by some fine cultural institutions.

New Yorkers, who have strong opinions on just about everything, generally consider the new marble-clad **Museum of Arts and Design** at 2 Columbus Circle to be a poor substitute for the fanciful Moorish tower from the 1960s that it replaces. The building gets more attention than the collection of crafts inside, which is a shame, because the contemporary glass pieces by Dale Chihuly, vintage Tiffany jewelry, and other pieces are stunning. So are the views over Columbus Circle and Central Park from **Robert**, the museum's sophisticated contemporary restaurant, open for lunch and dinner, as well as cocktails.

No one has much bad to say about **Jazz at Lincoln Center**, a cluster of nightclubs, performance halls, rehearsal stages, and recording studios tucked above the city in the glitzy Time-Warner Center, on the west side of the circle. You can hear the jazz canon in the 1,200-seat **Rose Theater**; in the smaller **Allen Room**, where floor-to-ceiling windows overlooking the city are the backdrop; or **Dizzy's Club Coca-Cola**, a swanky cabaret.

Back on terra firma, take a look at some of New York's most formidable statuary. Christopher Columbus stands atop a 70-foot-tall granite column in the middle of the circle, and the white-marble Maine Monument commemorates the Spanish American War and marks one of the main entrances to Central Park.

Museum of Arts and Design, 2 Columbus Circle; tel: 212-299-7777; www.madmuseum.org; Tue–Sun 11am–6pm, Thur until 9pm; charge; map E5 Jazz at Lincoln Center, 33 W. 60th St; tel: 212 258-9800; www.jalc.org; map D5

Indulge in international **epicurean delights** on a stroll up **Ninth Avenue**

The very name of Hell's Kitchen, once the city's hotbed of gangs and gangsters, used to send shivers up the spines of law-abiding citizens. Today a mention of the neighborhood is likely to get the taste buds watering. On a walk through Hell's Kitchen on and around Ninth Avenue from 40th and 59th streets you'll encounter an international smorgasbord of delicious offerings almost every step of the way. Many of the street's eateries are simple storefronts, and just about all serve on the premises and offer takeout as well.

So, take your pick. Greek? Consider the fried Cretan meatballs at **Uncle Nick's** (747 Ninth Ave at 51st St), creamy spreads at **Kashkaval** (856 Ninth Ave at 56th St), and heavenly baklava at **Poseidon Bakery** (629 Ninth Ave at 44th St). Middle Eastern? **Azuri Café** (465 W. 51st St, near Tenth Ave) makes the city's best shwarma sandwich, and **Gazala's Place** (709 Ninth Ave at 49th St) specializes in *chak choka*, eggs sautéed over garlic, onion, and tomato, and other dishes from the Druse sect. Latin? **Empanada Mama** (763 Ninth Ave at 51st St) makes dozens of varieties of the Mexican snack, and **Rice & Beans** (744 Ninth Ave at 50th St), true to its name, sticks to simple and delicious variations of Brazilian staples. Among the many places to satisfy a sweet tooth are **Ruby et Violette** (457 W. 50th St) for delectable chocolate chip cookies, **Little Pie Company** (424 W. 43rd St) for sour cream apple walnut pie and other desserts, and **Amy's** (672 Ninth Ave at 46th St) for perfect brownies and breads. Among the many excellent grocery stores, **Ninth Avenue International Foods** (543 Ninth Ave at 40th St) is piled high with Middle Eastern spices and Greek olives and cheeses.

Stands brimming with all this ethnic bounty fill the avenue during the annual Ninth Avenue Street Festival in May (www. hellskitchen.biz).

Hell's Kitchen; map C4

Chelsea, Flatiron, and Gramercy

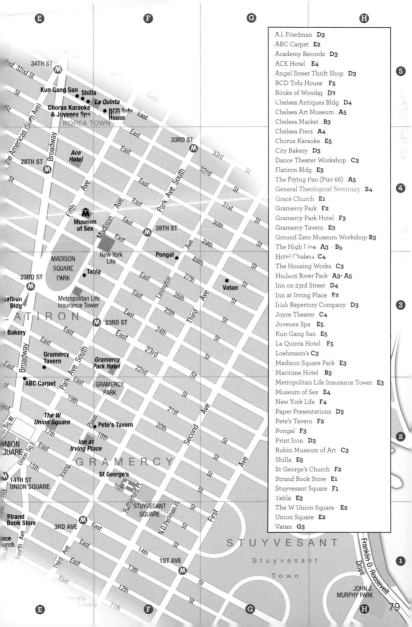

Find the spirit of bohemian New York at the **Hotel Chelsea** and tuck into a plate of **lobster paella**

The floors may be warped in places, many rooms have no views, there are no hairdryers or extra towels, and some complain the place is downright creepy, but no hotel in New York City can claim the bohemian artistic heritage of the **Hotel Chelsea.** Long-term residents included Leonard Cohen, Janis Joplin, Dylan Thomas, Arthur Miller, and Arthur C. Clarke (who wrote *2001: A Space Odyssey* here); the place was a favorite haunt of Patti Smith, Stanley Kubrick, Robert Mapplethorpe, and Jean-Paul Sartre. Andy Warhol shot *Chelsea Girls* here in 1966, documenting the lives of Factory alumni living here, such as Edie Sedgwick, and the 1986 film *Sid and Nancy* depicts the murder of Nancy Spungen by Sid Vicious in their room on the ground floor in 1978. The general public isn't allowed past the lobby, so taking an inexpensive room is the best way to explore the place – the grand staircase stretches up 12 flights, its walls are lined with art by guests and visitors, and the dark corridors with spots of peeling paint feel as though they belong in a state mental institution. Not for everyone, but a treat for the culturally inclined.

Old New York also lives next door to the Hotel Chelsea at the Spanish restaurant **El Quijote**, serving plates piled high with lobster and seafood paella along with pitchers of first-rate sangria in a traditional decor that feels like Madrid circa 1955. Don't expect first-rate service here, but instead enjoy a glimpse of old-school New York in one of the few traditional Spanish restaurants left in the city.

Hotel Chelsea, 222 W. 23rd St; tel: 212-243-3700; www.hotelchelsea.com; map C4
El Quijote, 226 W. 26th St; tel: 212 929-1855; map C4

Seek out **contemporary culture** and the home of a **Christmas legend**

Chelsea's scene encompasses more than gay life on the popular Eighth Avenue strip and the art galleries around Tenth Avenue (p. 83). The **Irish Repertory Company** (132 W. 22nd St, tel: 212-727-2737, www.irishrep.org, map D3), in a former warehouse, stages Irish and Irish-American works; the **Dance Theater Workshop** (219 W. 19th St, tel: 212-924-0077, www.dancetheaterworkshop. org; map C3) presents more than 110 performance by some 45 companies and performers every year; and the **Joyce Theater** (175 Eighth Ave, tel: 212-242-0800, www. joyce.org, map C4), in a renovated 1941 art film house, hosts international dance companies.

A bit farther west, the neighborhood turns its back on contemporary culture and is cloaked in the 19th century.

Cushman Row, as 20th Street between Eighth and Ninth avenues is known, recalls a more genteel era of real-estate development: a block of Greek Revival houses, built by speculators in 1840, are richly embellished with ornate windows and elaborate ironwork. The tree-shaded lawns of the **General Theological Seminary** (*pictured*; 21st St, between Ninth and Tenth aves, map B4), a block beyond, provide one of the city's most delightful retreats. Clement Clarke Moore, professor of Oriental and Greek Literature at Columbia University, left his mark in more ways than one. He donated part of his estate (named Chelsea) to the seminary. He also wrote *Twas the Night Before Christmas*, a poem that is still in the repertoire of all kids awaiting the arrival of Santa Claus on Christmas Eve.

Delight in the gourmet offerings of **Chelsea Market**

Market. Purveyors of some of the city's most delectable foodstuffs operate in the market, and on a stroll through the main food court you will encounter baked goods (Amy's Breads, Sarabeth's, and Eleni's), Italian cheeses and pastas (Buon Italia), wine (the Chelsea Wine Vault), kitchen wares (Bowery Kitchen Supply), and much more. You can enjoy your selections at tables and benches throughout the market.

The former factory floors upstairs are occupied by several television studios, including, appropriately, the Food Network.

Chelsea Market, Mon–Fri 7am–8pm, Sat 7am–7pm, Sun 8am–6pm; map B3

The block of Ninth Avenue between 15th and 16th streets has long been beloved in culinary circles. From the 1890s, the brick complex housed the Nabisco cookie factory. The famous Oreo was invented here in 1912, and huge ovens turned out billions of the cream-filled sandwich cookies over the next half-century.

These days the twisting, brick-walled hallways, decorated here and there with gears and other artifacts from the former factory, are home to Chelsea

> **A CHELSEA MARKET ALTERNATIVE**
> Essex Street Market, on the Lower East Side at 120 Essex Street (map p.132, C3), was created in 1940 as part of a scheme to clear city streets of pushcarts and stalls that were blocking traffic and hindering police and fire vehicles. The market became a gathering spot for the Lower East Side's Italian and Jewish residents, and after recent renovation, is once again filled with stalls selling meat, fish, fruit, vegetables, cheese, and delicious baked goods. The market is open Mon–Sat 8am–7pm.

Check out the **Chelsea gallery scene**

The blocks of far West Chelsea, around Tenth and Eleventh avenues, have never been terribly hospitable, a grid of dark, untidy streets lined with grimy warehouses, printing houses, taxi garages, and factories. This urban setting, especially the blocks between 20th and 26th streets, is these days the world's epicenter of contemporary art, home to more than 200 galleries. Chelsea galleries tend to be a bit snooty – they do not as a rule go out of their way to extend a warm welcome. Even so, stepping in and out of these spaces is a quintessential New York experience and an illuminating introduction to the current art scene. Arm yourself with a free Gallery Guide (available at any gallery) and the Art Guide, with detailed listings, published every Friday in the *New York Times*. Your tour should include the building at 529 West 20th Street, where dozens of galleries are spread over nine floors, and the block of West 24th Street between 10th and 11th avenues, a line-up of some of the city's finest galleries, including **Gladstone Gallery** (515), **Metro Pictures** (519), **Mary Boone Gallery** (541), and **Gagosian Gallery** (555).

You'll encounter another art work on West 22nd Street between 10th and 11th avenues. Trees growing along the sidewalk were planted by German artist Joseph Beuys – a welcome presence on these harsh city streets.

Most Chelsea galleries are open Tue–Sat 10am–6pm; map B5

Savor old New York around **Gramercy Park**

Gramercy Park is the city's most elitist greensward. Only those fortunate enough to live on the periphery of the square block of trees and gardens are allowed beyond the locked gates. Even so, millions of less privileged New Yorkers who can only peer through the iron fence don't seem to mind, and they speak proudly of the refuge from which they are excluded as one of the city's great treasures.

Irving Place, a remarkably well-preserved bastion of Old New York, runs south from the park to 14th Street. The handsome street, lined in part with refined brownstones, is forever linked with two literary New Yorkers. Washington Irving, author of *The Legend of Sleepy Hollow* and *Rip Van Winkle*, lent his name to the street, but claims that he lived in the Washington Irving House, at 17th Street, are unfounded. The house was, however, home to a famous turn-of-the-20th-century lesbian couple, Elisa de Wolfe, an actress and interior designer, and Elisabeth Marbury, a powerful literary agent. Their salon, where Sarah Bernhardt was likely to rub shoulders with Astors and Vanderbilts, was well known.

O. Henry merely drank on the street, at nearby **Pete's Tavern** (*pictured*). He penned some of America's favorite short stories in the dark, woody interior, where he seems to have found the muse for his warm, witty depictions of late 19th- and early 20th-century life. Take a seat in Pete's and ponder Irving's magic-infused stories of early America in these atmospheric old environs.

Pete's Tavern, 121 E. 18th St; tel: 212-473-7676; map F2

Get some interior inspiration at **ABC Carpet** and indulge in a chic sweet at **City Bakery**

Decor aficionados salivate at the thought of a shopping spree at **ABC Carpet** (preferably if someone else is picking up the tab). This boho-luxury furniture and home wares emporium is a New York institution known to induce fevers in those vulnerable to sticker shock, but it is unparalleled in its ability to inspire interior designer wannabes. Walk the creaky floors in this high-ceilinged Beaux-Arts building, and explore six levels of furniture, linen, house wares, and electronics. The furniture is both new and antique, ranging from industrial, Danish modern, 18th-century French, and Asian to modern retailers like Mitchell Gold & Bob Williams or Ralph Lauren. There are real finds here from around the world, such as Venetian chandeliers from Murano glass factories, Indonesian wedding beds, organic towels and linens, and, of course, piles and piles of carpets of all sizes, colors, and origins at the satellite store across the street at 881 Broadway – ABC Carpet is above all, the largest carpet and rug retailer in the world.

When you've reached design saturation, head to **City Bakery** for the best salad bar in the city, or for one of their signature pick-me-ups, such as the pretzel croissant or their rich, thick hot chocolate with a homemade giant marshmallow. The salad bar serves Asian-inspired dishes (Thai saffron rice with Lotus seeds; pesto soba noodle salad; grilled pineapple with ancho chili) or yummy comfort food like mac & cheese, or red bean and tomato stew with chipotle and lime. Take a seat on the main floor, or look down at the bustling crowd from upstairs in this large airy space with an industrial feel.

ABC Carpet, 888 Broadway; map E2
City Bakery, 3 W. 18th St; map D3

Poke through produce at the **Union Square Greenmarket**

Times Square bills itself as the Crossroads of the World, but for New Yorkers, **Union Square** is the crossroads of the city. The parcel is New York's version of London's Hyde Park Corner (the square has always been a rallying point) and Rome's Campo de' Fiori (the perimeter is the locale of New York's most popular outdoor market). While Union Square is not nearly as attractive as these European counterparts, it is appealingly animated around the clock, surrounded as it is by some of the city's liveliest neighborhoods. The message to be gleaned from a temperance fountain, into which Charity empties a jug of water, is lost on passersby making their way to and from the many nearby bars in Chelsea, Greenwich Village, and Gramercy Park. Some of the square's most eager habituées are shoppers who poke through piles of produce brought into the city from surrounding farmlands; with baskets and totes in hand, they approach their selections with the zeal of Provençal matrons.

Few of those who pass through the square are aware of the presence of some of the city's noblest statuary. From their perches, George Washington, Abraham Lincoln, and Mahatma Gandhi enjoy an enviable overview of goings-on in the city's most energetic public arena.

Union Square; map E2

> ### GREENMARKETS
> The **Union Square Greenmarket** is open Mon, Wed, Fri, and Sat, 8am–6pm; in addition to locally grown fruits and vegetables, vendors sell cheeses, artisan breads, jams, and other bounty. You will also find greenmarkets at many other locations around the city, including: First Ave between 92nd and 93rd streets, Sun 9am–5pm; Columbus Ave between 77th and 79th streets, Sun 8am–4pm; 97th St between Columbus and Amsterdam aves, Fri 8am–2pm; and 57th St at Ninth Ave, Wed and Sat 9am–2pm.

Discover **Tibetan art and vintage bargains** on Thrift Shop Row

For a unique museum experience, tour the compact and refined **Rubin Museum of Art**, considered the most important museum of Himalayan art in the Western world. The temporary exhibits are laid out thematically ('The Tibetan Art of the Afterlife', 'The Art of the Katmandu Valley'), with detailed descriptions that do a great job explaining the rich philosophies and culture of this 1,800-mile mountainous region that runs from Afghanistan in the north to Myanmar in the south. The six-story museum has more than 2,000 objects and works of art, including a huge collection of female Buddhas and stunning Mandalas. The curators like to keep things interesting here: they host a dynamic and imaginative program of screenings, lectures, and concerts with themes connected to Buddhist and Himalayan thought or spirit. Talks with notable experts have included 'What makes the mindset of a radical?' or 'Are we hard-wired for worship?' Friday night films (free with a $7 drink purchase at the bar) include the 1975 adaptation of Bertolt Brecht's *Galileo*, and concerts have featured guitar-wiz Willy Porter, Roxanne Cash, or Harlem jazz inspired by Himalayan art in the museum.

To keep in a spiritual mindset, spend some money on Thrift Shop Row further along West 17th Street, where **The Housing Works** (143) and **Angel Thrift Shop** (118) sell quality vintage clothes and household goods, the proceeds going to sufferers from HIV/AIDS or mental illness. The Housing Works (dubbed 'Salvation Armani') is known for its creative window displays, designer castoffs at tiny prices, and online auctions of choice jewelry, furniture, and books. The Angel Street Thrift Shop often receives donations from well-known designers and furniture companies.

Rubin Museum of Art, W. 17th St at Seventh Ave; tel: 212-620-5000; www.rmanyc.org; Mon, Thur 11am–5pm, Wed 11am–7pm, Fri 11am–10pm, Sat 11am–6pm, closed Tue; charge; map C3

Take the high road on **the High Line**, a sanctuary from the city bustle, **by day and by night**

Not too much gets a unanimous nod of approval from New Yorkers, but the High Line is one of those rare exceptions. Just about everyone seems to have something good to say about this elevated promenade, a refreshing strip of greenery that cuts an aerial swath through the heart of Chelsea, between Tenth and Eleventh avenues all the way from Gansevoort Street to 30th Street.

The High Line is a disused railway trestle that once handled train traffic up and down the West Side, a supply route for factories and warehouses. Fountains, patches of greenery (some cultivated from the wild plants that took root on the abandoned tracks), and benches line the route, reached by staircases from the streets below.

As you follow the High Line you can peer down into the

Meatpacking District and other old industrial neighborhoods below. At 17th Street, the view south extends all the way across New York Harbor to the Statue of Liberty. At 18th Street, the Empire State Building looms into view. Some of New York's most exciting new architecture has risen around the High Line, including a curvaceous glass creation by Frank Gehry at Eleventh Avenue and 18th Street.

At sunset, an orange glow hangs over the Hudson River, and discreet lighting along the route ensures that the night sky, enlivened here and there with a faint star, provides a romantic canopy above the route. Weekday mornings the walkways are uncrowded, a quiet sanctuary as the workaday city rushes by below.

The High Line; 7am–10pm daily; www. thehighline.org; map B3–5

Enjoy a cocktail in a glamorous lounge and dine like a sophisticate at the Gramercy Tavern

It's hard to not be impressed by the paintings by Cy Twombly, Andy Warhol, Jean-Michel Basquiat, Damien Hirst, and Richard Prince hanging at **The Gramercy Park Hotel**. They were chosen by artist and filmmaker Julian Schnabel, who masterminded a dramatic redesign of the lobby and bars of this historic hotel in 2003 when it was bought by former Studio 54 owner and hotel impresario Ian Schrager. The creative revamp succeeds in respecting the bohemian past of this legendary hotel (Humphrey Bogart and James Cagney lived here; Bob Dylan, The Clash, and David Bowie have stayed here) while injecting some modern high-end glamour. Today, the hotel attracts the moneyed international art set (Karl Lagerfeld and members of the Whitney family own apartments here), so settle in for some people-watching as you shoot some pool in the main lounge, or sip on a cocktail in an oversized armchair by the fire. And you're sure to overhear interesting conversation seated at the adjacent smaller bar.

Continue indulging in good taste and worldly sophistication at the **Gramercy Tavern** a few blocks away, a city favorite for drinks or a high-end meal. It is a cozy and refined spot, with its high ceilings, dark-wood beams, dramatic floral arrangements, subdued lighting, and mature buzz in the air. The bartenders are well informed and will help you choose the right wine or dish from the top-notch menu. Or, sit in the main dining area or in the more secluded (and expensive) back room and spoil yourself by ordering the gourmet tasting menu.

The Gramercy Park Hotel, 2 Lexington Ave at 21st St, see p.176; map F3 Gramercy Tavern, 42 E. 20th St; tel: 212-477-0777; www.gramercytavern.com; map E3

Swing a golf club in January or skate indoors in July at **Chelsea Piers**

The **Chelsea Piers Sports and Entertainment Complex** is a sprawling 30-acre sports village on the Hudson River that offers year-round golf, skating, rock-climbing, bowling, and intensive sports training. This is where luxury transatlantic liners would arrive and depart from 1910-30 (the *Titantic* was scheduled to dock here, but instead it became the drop-off point for its rescued lifeboats). Today, the piers house the city's largest training center for gymnastics, two basketball courts, a bowling alley, fields for soccer and lacrosse, as well as a golf club, two full-sized skating rinks, and film, TV, and photo studios.

The **golf club** (Pier 59; tel: 212-336-6400) has a multistoried driving range overlooking the river open year-round (the stalls are heated in winter), and lessons are available from PGA pros.

The only year-round **skating rinks** (Pier 61; tel: 212-336-6100) in the city are open for general skating daily in the afternoons. Indoor **baseball batting cages** (between Piers 61 and 62; tel: 212-336-6500) with different pitching speeds can be rented for half-hour or hour-long sessions. **300 bowling** (between Piers 59 and 60; tel: 212-835-2695) is a state-of-the-art 32-lane bowling alley, complete with cocktail bar, video screens, and a grill menu.

After flexing your muscles, treat yourself to a massage or a sauna at **The Spa** (Pier 60; tel: 212-336-6780), or enjoy a beer at the **Chelsea Brewing Company** (Pier 59; tel: 212-336-6440), the only microbrewery in Manhattan, which makes 20 handcrafted brews right on the premises, with a view of the river and the golf driving range.

Chelsea Piers between 17th and 23rd streets and the West Side Highway; www.chelseapiers.com; map A4

Be a night owl in **K Town**

The city that never sleeps is especially nocturnal in Korea Town, as 32nd Street between Sixth and Fifth avenues is known. On the block-long strip you can dig into Korean barbecue, sing karaoke, or soak in a spa around the clock.

In dozens of restaurants, *galbi* (thinly sliced beef short ribs), *jeyook gui* (broiled pork), *bugogi* (sirloin), *saeoo gae* (jumbo shrimp), and other specialties are prepared at your table – either grilled over coals or sautéed on a hot griddle. Accompaniments are *bibimbop* (rice and vegetables) and *bi bim naeng myun* (noodles topped with kimchi, or pickled vegetables). Among the favorite places on the street to enjoy these delicacies are **Shilla** (37 W. 32nd St, tel: 212-967-1880), with a three-story tall dining room; **Kum Gang San** (49 W 32nd, tel: 212-967-0909), enlivened by a stunning waterfall; and **BCD Tofu House** (17 W. 32nd St, tel: 212-967-1900), where a hearty tofu stew is the house specialty.

Wherever you dine, and whatever you order, you will probably wash down your meal with *soju*, a clear, potent liquor that looks and tastes quite a bit like vodka. After a few glasses you will be well primed to partake of

K Town's other great diversion, karaoke. The neighborhood's two most popular venues are **Chorus Karaoke** (25 W. 32nd St, tel: 212-967-2244), and **Duet 35** (53 W. 35th St, tel: 646-473-0827).

Should these exertions wear you out, the **Juvenix Spa** (25 W. 32nd St, fifth floor) is open at all hours to provide a sweat in a sauna made of semiprecious stones and a soak in a tub filled with sake, tea, and algae. If the weather is good, and midnight has not yet struck, you might want to make a stop at **La Quinta Inn** (17 W. 32nd St). Ascend to the Sun Roof, a pleasant aerie where cocktails are served until midnight – when the night is still young in this 24-hour neighborhood.

Korea Town; map E5

Ponder human sexuality at the **Museum of Sex** then watch flirtation in action at a lively **outdoor bar**

The Museum of Sex takes the subject seriously: its board of advisers is filled with historians and scholars, and the museum's goal is to show the best in current thinking about human sexuality. Academic purpose aside, the exhibits are fun and informative, such as 'Rubbers: the Life, History, and Struggle of the Condom', 'Graphic Sex in Japan,' and 'Sex and the Moving Image.' The museum has more than 15,000 artifacts related to subjects of human sexuality, and houses a research and multimedia library. The explicit nature of the material, however, means admittance is restricted to those 18 and older.

To see the human mating game in real life on a warm day, head to the **Frying Pan**, a 1929 lightship tethered to Pier 66 at West 26th Street and the West Side Highway. The boat and the pier have been converted into a large bustling bar and casual eating spot, where buckets of Corona, burgers, and clams are served up with a fabulous view of the Hudson River. Plastic chairs are on deck, the interior is barnacle-encrusted with worn couches, an exposed engine room, and bands or DJs playing on occasion in the belly of the boat. Those prone to seasickness are counseled to remain on dry land and enjoy the Tiki Bar.

In winter months, the artistic crowd in the neighborhood packs **The Breslin Bar** in the trendy Ace Hotel (see p.170). Wood flooring, high ceilings, and a vintage mahogany bar give this gastro pub an old-world, gentleman's club feel, respectful of the hotel's 1904 origins.

Museum of Sex, 233 Fifth Ave at 28th St; tel: 212-689-6337; www.museumofsex. com; 11am–6.30pm, Sun–Fri, Sat 11am–8pm; map E4
The Frying Pan, Pier 66 at W. 26th St; tel: 212-989-6363; May–Oct; map A5

Indulge in paper and craft products in **the 'Paper District'** on West 18th Street

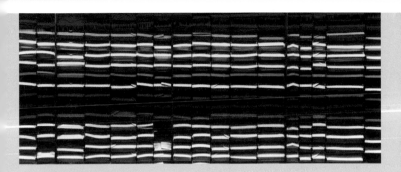

The digital world seems far way on West 18th Street between Fifth and Sixth avenues: three shops here specialize in paper for invitations, projects, presentations, wrapping, and letters, and tucked in the middle of the block is the city's best children's bookstore.

Paper Presentation (no. 23) and **Print Icon** (no. 7) are both paradise for graphic designers and creative types, selling paper and envelopes in all colors, sizes, and textures, along with services for printing stationery, invitations, or business cards. Print Icon is the printer of choice for ad agencies and graphic designers working in the area, and you can watch the presses roll at the back of the shop. Paper Presentation has everything for the scrap-booker and card-designer: watch you don't get lost in a creative fog

going through the huge choice of stickers, glitter, ribbons, pens, markers, and rubber stamp pads. **A. I. Friedman**'s shop (no. 44) runs the width of a city block, and sells paper, agendas, picture frames and albums, art portfolios, interesting messenger bags, and office furniture.

For a great selection of classic and new children's books, pop into **Books of Wonder** (no. 19), the oldest and largest independent children's bookstore in the city, specializing in children's literature, with its own cute cafe serving brightly decorated cakes and cookies. Classical music fans will love **Academy Records and CDs** a couple of doors down (no. 12), the city's best source for used classical, jazz, and showtune LPs and CDs.

The Paper District, W. 18th St; map D3

Greenwich Village and the Meatpacking District

Enjoy the views along the **Hudson River** from a bike, a pier, or hanging from a trapeze

Over the past decade, more than $400 million have been poured into converting industrial land and abandoned piers along the Hudson River into the **Hudson River Park** (www.hudsonriverpark.org) a 5½-mile stretch of parks, bike and pedestrian paths, tennis and basketball courts, and places to fish or launch a kayak. It's quickly become a favorite escape for nature-starved, stressed-out New Yorkers and tourists. The paths run from Battery Park up to 59th Street, passing more than half a dozen converted piers with green space, outdoor theaters, and benches. But most New Yorkers agree the best stretch lies below 23rd Street.

Pier 45 (map A3) is perfect for lying out on the grass and taking in a rare sense of open space. Enjoy the views of the Statue of Liberty and the New Jersey shoreline,

a sunset, or watch the river traffic ballet of police and tourist helicopters, tugboats, cruise-ships, and kayaks. The last can be rented for free for 20-minute trips further south at the **Downtown Boathouse, Pier 40** (www.downtownboathouse.org, Sat–Sun 9am–6pm, map A2), life jackets and brief instruction provided.

For intrepid individuals looking for an upside-down view of the Hudson River, the **New York Trapeze School** offers 2-hour lessons for about $50–60, also at Pier 40 (tel: 212-242-TSNY; www.newyork.trapezeschool.com; map A2).

But one of the best ways to enjoy the new park is on two wheels. **Bike rentals** are available in Midtown from **Pier 84** at 44th Street (www.bikeandroll.com) or at **Battery Park** (map p.150 B1).

Relax in **St Luke's Gardens** and spot dozens of species of butterflies and birds

Tucked away off Hudson Street around the historic Church of St Luke in the Fields is **St Luke's Gardens**, a warren of small green spaces linked by paths which is home to dozens of species of migrating birds and butterflies, blossoming cherry trees in spring, a rose garden, century-old maple trees, and wooden benches for contemplating it all.

These 3 acres of walkways, lawns, and rare plants form one of the more distinctive gardens in the city, in part thanks to the warm microclimate created by the gardens' southwest orientation and the heat-retaining brick walls surrounding them. Over the years 100 types of birds have been spotted here, as well as 24 types of moths and butterflies, drawn to the berries and flowers planted here.

Enter by the south gate adjacent to the church and follow the paths to secluded areas. One is a small lawn, surrounded by trees and shrubs selected to attract the birds and butterflies. Around the corner from there is an alleyway, planted with 22 cherry trees that blossom in pink and white in mid-April. There are benches throughout, the perfect place to contemplate the greenery and enjoy a coffee or a book.

The gardens are part of the Episcopal St Luke's School and Church, built in 1820 and the third-oldest church in New York, dedicated to the physician evangelist, in recognition of the Village's role as a refuge from yellow-fever epidemics. One of the founding wardens of the church was Clement Clarke Moore, a gentleman scholar of biblical Hebrew and Greek who also penned *Twas the Night before Christmas*.

St Luke in the Fields, 487 Hudson St; map B3

Take in the vibe at a **Village jazz joint**

These days, Greenwich Village is more upscale enclave than bohemian mecca, but many jazz clubs that opened in the 1960s and even in the '20s are still going strong, largely thanks to dedicated owners who believe passionately in the cause.

The jazz club that many jazz fans call the greatest in the world is **The Village Vanguard** (178 Seventh Ave South, tel: 212-255-4037, map C4) where Miles Davis, Charles Mingus, John Coltrane, and Thelonious Monk all played and recorded. The low ceilings and shape of the room make for great acoustics, and its high professional standards have been kept intact since 1935. The space is cramped and a little dingy, but the $30-or-so ticket price (including two drinks)

is lower than other high-end jazz clubs like the **Blue Note** (131 W. 3rd St, tel: 212-475-8592, map D3) nearby, which also hosts top-of-the-line shows but with a feel that's more nightclub than jazz joint.

Originally a speakeasy in the 1920s, the unpretentious **55 Bar** (55 Christopher St, tel: 212-929-9883, map C4) is one of the best-kept music secrets in the city. The cover charge ranges from free to $12 for two sets, the drinks are cheap, and musicians love to play here. The up-and-coming jazz, R&B, and jazz-world-folk crossover bands rarely disappoint thanks to the high standards of the owner who runs the club more for creative satisfaction than for profits.

Other authentic places include **Small's** (183 West 10th St, tel: 212-252-5091, map C4), known for its jams into the wee hours, or **Cornelia Street Café** (29 Cornelia St, tel: 212-989-9319, map C3). For top-end experimental jazz, check out **Le Poisson Rouge** (158 Bleecker St, tel: 212-505-3474, map D2). And for a great traditional jazz brunch go to **North Square** (103 Waverly Place, tel: 212-254-1200, map D3) at the Washington Square Hotel, to hear seasoned New York jazz vocalists such as Roz Corral.

Step back into the '60s and the **Village folk scene**

The last cultural hey-day of Greenwich Village was the folk era of the early 1960s, when Bob Dylan crashed onto the international stage, getting his start in small clubs and writing songs in his Village walk-up apartment. Today, most of the traces of that era are gone, but a few remain more or less intact.

The corner of Jones and West 4th Street is a bit like the Abbey Road of Dylan's career: this is where the cover photo of *Freewheelin'* was taken one wintry February afternoon in 1963 with then-girlfriend Suze Rotolo. The two shared an apartment on the top floor of **161 West 4th Street** a block away. Dylan and other folkies such as Peter, Paul & Mary, Pete

Seeger, and Joan Baez would pop into **The Music Inn** a few doors down at no. 169. Here they'd buy or borrow guitars, violins, and rhythm instruments from the owner who is still there today, tucked in the basement repairing and hand-making instruments. The upstairs is jammed-packed with mandolins, guitars, bongos, sitars, and world instruments of all kinds. The window display looks like it hasn't been touched since the '60s, and the place is not recommended for the claustrophobic.

Big names in folk music and rock have bought new and used guitars at **Matt Umanov** for decades. The selection is impressive, and the sales help highly informed. Suze Rotolo's son works here.

Everyone from Woody Allen to George Carlin, Janis Joplin, Dylan, and even Frank Zappa have played at some point at **The Bitter End**. It's the last club of the folk era still going strong, programming six acts a night.

Music Inn World Instruments, 169 W. 4th St; tel: 212-243-5715; map D3
Matt Umanov Guitars, 273 Bleecker St; tel: 212-675-2157; map C3
The Bitter End, 147 Bleecker St; tel: 212-673-7030; www.bitterend.com; map D2

Bask in **a bibliophile's paradise**, then embark on **a literary tour**

It may be small, but many New Yorkers say **Three Lives** (154 W. 10th St, map D4) is the best bookstore in the city. In his Pulitzer Prize-winning novel, *The Hours*, writer Michael Cunningham calls it 'the most civilized place on earth.' There's a good selection of noteworthy new non-fiction and fiction, and a thorough choice of respected titles on the shelves. The staff are friendly and informed, and the atmosphere cozy. Browsing here is a book-lover's dream.

The Strand (828 Broadway, map F3) and its '18 Miles of Books' is one of the biggest and best-used bookstores in America. Negotiating your way among browsers and big tables piled high with books can try your patience, but most find it hard to leave without making a purchase.

The literary pedigree of Greenwich Village is undisputed. Over the last two centuries, the neighborhood has played a key role in American literature and is peppered with literary landmarks. Here are some to look out for:

The New School for Social Research (66 W. 12th St, map E4) opened in 1919 as a place for professors considered too liberal for the then-stiflingly traditional Columbia University. In the 1930s, it became a sort of university-in-exile for intellectuals fleeing Nazi Germany. Writers who have taught here include Joseph Heller, Edward Albee, WH Auden, Robert Frost, Joyce Carol Oates, Arthur Miller, and Susan Sontag.

Patchin Place (map D4) is a pretty mews where e. e. cummings lived from 1923–62, entertaining the likes of TS Eliot, Ezra Pound, and Dylan Thomas. Djuna Barnes spent the last 40 years of her somewhat reclusive life here. In the early 1960s Edward Albee bought a converted carriage house at **50 West 10th Street** (map D4) where he wrote Pulitzer Prize-winning plays including *A Delicate Balance*. Historic watering hole **The White Horse Tavern** (567 Hudson St, map B4), where Dylan Thomas had his infamous drinking spree a couple of days before he went most un-gentle into that good night, is today a favourite among students and assorted literati. At 9½ feet in width, **75½ Bedford Street** is the narrowest house in the Village, and was home to poet Edna St Vincent Malley from 1923–25. She also founded the **Cherry Lane Theatre** (*pictured*, 38 Commerce St, map C3) just around the corner, where Samuel Beckett's *Waiting for Godot* was first staged. A little further east at **no. 11**, Washington Irving wrote *The Legend of Sleepy Hollow* in 1931.

Other literary landmarks in the neighbourhood include **7 Washington Square North** (map E3) home to Edith Wharton in 1882, while **no. 19** was the home of Henry James's grandmother and a setting of his novel *Washington Square Park*; Louisa May Alcott lived at **130-132 MacDougal Street** (map D2) and penned *Little Women* here in 1880. In the 1930s and '40s, the nearby **Minetta Tavern** (113 MacDougal St, map D2), which began as a speakeasy became a favorite haunt among local luminaries. Following a Keith 'Midas Touch' McNally revamp, the picture-perfect brasserie is now a buzzing, fashionable (and hard to get into) restaurant.

Spot celebrities in and around **Waverly Place**

There are perhaps more well-known actors, celebrities, and writers living in the leafy, peaceful West Village than in any other enclave in the city. So it can be easy to spot one if you keep your eyes peeled. Julianne Moore, Liv Tyler *(pictured below at the Waverly Inn)*, Sarah Jessica Parker, and Matthew Broderick are a few of the well-known people who live in the beautiful townhouses lining Greenwich Village streets.

If you'd like to increase your odds of spotting a celebrity, try to get a table at the exclusive **Waverly Inn.** Owned by *Vanity Fair* editor Graydon Carter, this uber-hip restaurant has pulled in media moguls, Hollywood stars, and other assorted A-listers since it opened several years ago. It can be tough to get a reservation – there's no phone, and front-of-house management is discerning.

Instead, try getting a seat at the small bar when the restaurant opens at 6pm, or past 11pm when the dinner crowds begin to thin. Be warned, the drinks are not cheap. You'll always know the celebrity power inside by the number of paparazzi hanging around outside.

Another place to spot celebrities, fashionistas, and power-players, is Keith McNally's **Morandi**, just a few blocks away. In the warmer months, the terrace of this rustic Italian restaurant overflows with the tanned and beautiful, and a quick scan often produces a celebrity sighting. Sarah Jessica Parker, Matthew Modine, and Cameron Diaz have all been spotted having breakfast or lunch here during the day when things are quieter.

French Roast nearby is also a favorite among celebrities for its relaxed and unpretentious atmosphere. Recent sightings include David Byrne, Sean Lennon, an Olsen twin, and Gabriel Byrne.

Waverly Inn, 16 Bank St at Waverly Place; no phone; map C4
Morandi; 211 Waverly Place; tel: 212-627-7575; map D4
French Roast, 78 W. 11th St at Sixth Ave; tel: 212-533-2233; map D4

Do some **people-watching** and listen to music in **Washington Square Park**

Following a $16 million renovation, the newly spruced-up Washington Square Park is now a pleasant spot to sit on a bench with a paper and maybe a spot of lunch, listen to music, and enjoy the ebb and flow of Villagers, bohemians, tourists, students and academics from surrounding NYU buildings, workers on breaks, and local residents with their dogs.

If you're lucky, you'll be there when the fragrant food cart of Sri Lankan-born Thiru Kumar is parked on the south edge of the park at Sullivan Street (Mon–Fri 11am–4pm, but times can vary depending on the weather). His mild or spicy *dosas* are praised by foodies across the city.

The park has been a draw for musicians since World War II, when folkies would gather near the fountain on weekend afternoons. Buddy Holly, Woodie Guthrie, and Bob Dylan have all jammed here over the years, and the tradition continues. Classical concerts are held in the northeast corner of the park in July, and Christmas caroling takes place around the arch in December.

In the southeast corner of the park, regular chess players do battle, while 'chess hustlers' take on passers by in an attempt to make a few bucks. On Sundays, champions from the National Scrabble Club gather here to compete.

Washington Square Park; map E3

Visit a **time capsule** of fashionable 19th-century life, then tap into the **Zeitgeist on the Bowery**

A great way to kick off a tour of New York's neighbourhood-of-the-moment is to get a glimpse of fashionable life in the 1800s at **Merchant's House** on East Fourth Street. This elegant red-brick row house was home to a prosperous merchant family, and today it's the only home in New York preserved intact from the mid-19th century, with much of the original furniture, decor, and family belongings still in place.

A block away is the Bowery, a once dodgy thoroughfare now home to some of the city's hippest new hotels and buzz-worthy restaurants. Have a drink at the

> **BOWERY BITES**
> Big-name chefs are now on the Bowery: Daniel Boulud's **DBGB's Kitchen and Bar** (299 Bowery, tel: 212-933-5300) – named in homage to the Bowery's defunct rock club CBGB's – features upscale burgers and sausages, while hit-making restaurateur Keith McNally has opened his latest rustic Italian, **Pulino's Bar and Pizzeria** (282 Bowery, tel: 212-226-1966) on this trendy stretch.

sleek downstairs bar at **Cooper Square Hotel** (*pictured*) or enjoy the intimacy of the upstairs bar with outdoor seating or great views through wall-to-ceiling windows.

Down the street is The Lobby Bar at the **Bowery Hotel**, where Ashton threw a birthday party for Demi, and Mark Anthony for J-Lo. Settle into oversized velvet chairs and take in the opulent French chateau hunting-lodge feel of the place with its marble fireplaces, wall-mounted antlers, and oriental carpets. The hotel's rustic restaurant Gemma is a good place for a casual meal or coffee.

Merchant's House, 29 E. 4th St; tel: 212-777-1089; www.merchantshouse.com; Mon, Thur–Sun, 12–5pm; map F2
Cooper Square Hotel (see p.170)
Bowery Hotel, 335 Bowery; tel: 212-505-9100; www.theboweryhotel.com; map F1

Judge the best **music at three Village churches** in the unofficial 'Battle of the Choirs and Organists'

Within just a few blocks, three of the city's most active churches offer music events, often free of charge. There's no real competition here of course, just a blessing for the music-loving public.

The Gothic Revival **Grace Church**, at the corner of Broadway and 11th Street, was built in 1843 by James Renwick Jr, later the architect of St Patrick's Cathedral uptown. The Episcopalian church is a national landmark – free tours take place Sundays at 1pm. But it's the music that makes Grace a draw for New Yorkers. It's famous for its men and boys choir, which sings during services and performs concerts in respected venues such as Carnegie Hall. Free organ meditations take place daily at noon. For a full music schedule, see the website.

A few blocks on, is the **Church of the Ascension**, also Episcopalian, which by the end of 2010 will house one of the premier organs in the world. The church is home to the Voices of Ascension, the Grammy Award-nominated professional choir who give concerts here, as well as at other venues around the city such as Lincoln Center and Carnegie Hall. The beautiful main sanctuary is being restored, and will open again to the public by late 2010.

One block north, the **First Presbyterian Church** of New York was built in 1846 after originating near Wall Street in 1716. The church is home to the Guilmant Organ School, one of the first accredited schools in America devoted to teaching organists and church musicians. Organ and choral recitals take place here throughout the year.

Grace Church, Broadway and 11th St; www.gracechurchnyc.org; map F3
Church of the Ascension, Fifth Ave and 10th St; www.assentionnyc.org; map E4
First Presbyterian Church, Fifth Ave and 11th St; www.fpcnyc.org; map E4

Sample cheeses and bite into fresh salami in the city's **'real'** Little Italy

Sadly, all that's left of the city's 'official' Little Italy located just north of Chinatown is an abundance of mediocre Italian restaurants and cafes geared at tourists. Manhattan's 'real' Little Italy is now confined to a stretch of Bleecker Street between Sixth and Seventh avenues, a hub of Italian immigration around the turn of the 20th century. Today, an authentic Italian feel remains thanks to an active Catholic church on the block, several Italian bakeries, butchers, and food shops, and one of the best pizzerias in the city. And with new gourmet shops opening up, the street is transforming itself into a downtown food destination.

Italian delicacies abound at **Faicco's Pork Store** (no. 260): fresh mozzarella, dozens of varieties of homemade sausage, prosciutto, and meats of all kinds sold at an old-fashioned counter, plus sandwiches and packaged heat-and-go meals like eggplant parmigiana or lasagna. Next door, **Murray's** (no. 254) is one of the best cheese shops in the city. The informed staff lets you taste-test a wide selection of cheeses from Italy, France, and many other countries. They hold cheese classes too. Traditional family butcher **Ottomanelli & Sons** (no. 285) has been in business for more than 80 years. Even if you don't want to buy a steak or a leg of lamb, it's fun to check out the old-style *ambiente*. For mouthwatering *cannoli* (pastries filled with sweet ricotta cream) or tiramisu along with a satisfying cup of espresso, take a seat at **Pasticceria Rocco** (no. 243). Some argue the best pizza in town is at **John's Pizzeria** (no. 278, tel: 212-243-1680). Make sure you're hungry – pizzas are made to order and sold by the pie, not the slice.

Bleecker St, between Sixth and Seventh Aves; map C3

Bag a comfy seat, order a latte, and **strike up a conversation** with a local in one of these **cool cafes**

The cafe **Doma**, meaning 'home' in Czech, is certainly home for many freelance scribblers, actors, filmmakers, and other creative types who use this cafe as a more spacious alterative to their tiny apartments nearby. Although often as quiet as a library (albeit a see-and-be-seen library, where eyes swoop to the door when it opens), the cafe has an unspoken rule that sitting at the central table means you're open to conversation – friendships, romances, and business deals have all sprouted here. Doma also serves light café fare (omelets, salads, and gourmet sandwiches), as well as wine and beer in the evenings.

Set in a former garage, **Grounded** is a more hipster alternative to Doma, priding itself on a post-hippie, lived-in feel with kitschy thrift-shop mugs, politically-correct coffee, and a soundtrack that alternates between '70s staples and current indie Brooklyn bands. Like Doma, Grounded has a social common area of wooden benches and a couch grouped around a coffee table, where it's acceptable to chat with the person next to you.

Joe's has won best cafe in the New York press because of the quality of the coffee, but the atmosphere isn't quite as enticing as at Doma or Grounded. It's smaller here, usually quite crowded, and the tables and chairs are less comfortable. However, getting a spot outside on one of two benches and watching activity on this pretty street is an ideal way to spend an hour or two on a warm day. There's a second Joe's by Union Square (9 E. 13th St), where it's easier to get a table.

Doma, 17 Perry St; map C4
Grounded, 28 Jane St; map C5
Joe's, 141 Waverly Place; map D3

Take in the buzz of the **Meatpacking District nightlife**

This once-seedy area, where gay bondage clubs and drug dealing dens rubbed shoulders with slaughterhouses and meatpackaging plants, has been fully transformed into a high-end fashionista's paradise. Designer boutiques line the streets, and at night the stylish hop in and out of cabs, expensive high heels clicking on cobblestones.

The main draw is the new **Standard Hotel** (see p.171), straddled over the southern end of the popular High Line park (p.88). If you can't get into the Standard Grill restaurant, throw back a pint or play ping-pong in the ground-floor Biergarten, or sip a cocktail in the quiet lobby bar looking out over the street. Eighteen floors up is the (pricey) penthouse Boom Boom Bar, with panoramic views of the city and the Hudson River.

Still going strong after more than a decade is Keith McNally's atmospheric **Pastis** (9 Ninth Ave, tel: 212 929-4844, map B5). Modeled after a French bistro circa 1958, it is full most nights. An equally successful themed restaurant is Jean-Georges Vongerichten's **Spice Market** (430 W. 13th St, tel: 212-675-2322, map B5), with its mouthwatering dishes inspired by Asian street food.

A more intimate atmosphere is a block away at **Macelleria** (48 Gansevoort St, tel: 212-741-2555, map B5), a rustic Italian restaurant with outdoor tables in warm weather, or a fun place for an outdoor drink is the terrace of **La Bodega** (363 W. 16th St, tel: 212-243-8400), in the still-trendy Maritime Hotel (see p.171).

Shop for **designer clothes** and munch on the icing-laden **cupcakes** of *Sex and the City* fame

The outer edges of Greenwich Village, known as the far West Village, were as recently as a decade ago a deserted, inhospitable area, the streets buffeted by cold winds off the Hudson River in winter, and visited by the spill-over of transvestite hookers from the neighboring Meatpacking District. The wholesale butchers and prostitutes are gone, and the only thing being slaughtered there these days are fashion victims by the prices of designer clothes by the likes of Stella McCartney and the late Alexander McQueen, whose shops along these cobblestoned roads have supplanted the warehouses.

This fashion mecca has spread to the more intimate Bleecker Street, turning the first few blocks of the north end of this central roadway from Bank Street to Christopher Street into a miniature Madison Avenue, lined with boutiques belonging to Ralph Lauren, Marc Jacobs, Lulu Guinness, Cynthia Rowley, and Coach.

The street has become a destination for the well-heeled on weekends, who when they need a sugar pick-me-up, head to **Magnolia Bakery** (401 Bleecker St; tel: 212-462-2572; map C4), a cupcake shop made famous by its appearance on *Sex and the City*, which triggered the national cupcake craze. There's usually a line up to a block long to get in, even late at night, but most say it's worth the wait for the icing-laden cupcakes and old-fashioned desserts like banana creme pie and ice-box cake.

While most of the stores along this high-end shopping corridor are luxury clothes retailers, there is the occasional good-value gem, like the small optical chain **See** (no. 312) which sells imaginative frames and lenses at low prices that can be ready for pick-up in a few days.

Shoot pool at Fat Cat and go for a strike at Bowlmor

Game-playing New Yorkers have a field day at **Fat Cat**, a vast subterranean games room which holds 10 pool tables, 10 ping-pong tables, along with half a dozen foosball and shuffleboard tables, chessboards, and a bar area where people can sit and play Scrabble or backgammon. The place is dark, crowded, and usually noisy, and adding to the energetic mayhem are jazz, soul, or Gospel bands playing on a small stage tucked to the side. Three groups play each night from 7pm–2am, with an informal jazz jam session taking over until closing at 4.30am. At night the place is generally packed with 20–30-year-olds and the NYU student set looking for an inexpensive and fun alternative to nightclubs and restaurants.

Bowlmor Lanes near Union Square is also a nighttime destination for New Yorkers looking for something different to do. The management at Bowlmor spiffed up a neglected three-floor bowling alley about a decade ago, turning it into a retro-hip spot with glow-in-the-dark bowling, big-screen videos, a huge sound system and a couple of bars. Some complain both the drinks and the bowling are too expensive ($24 for shoes and unlimited bowling from 9pm–1am), but others counter that the place is well managed and conveniently located.

Fat Cat, 75 Christopher St at Seventh Ave; tel: 212-675-6056; map C4
Bowlmor Lanes, 110 University Place; tel: 212-255-8188; map F4

Enjoy a meal in a cozy **Greenwich Village eatery**

One of the main draws of Greenwich Village is the vast choice of intimate restaurants tucked along the picturesque streets. Here are a few favorites:

The Cornelia Street Café (29 Cornelia St, tel: 212-989-9319, map C3) is a busy, cozy, comforting Franco-American restaurant with a solid and affordable menu (duck confit with lentils, seafood stew) and a jazz and folk club downstairs.

Trendy gastro-pub **The Spotted Pig** (*pictured*, 314 11th St, tel: 212-620-0393, map B4) is open late and always full. The $20 charbroiled burger with blue cheese is a favorite.

Pearl Oyster Bar (18 Cornelia St, tel: 212-691-8211, map C3) is a highly rated seafood restaurant and packs in crowds every night. The straightforward dishes (lobster rolls, scallops, and oysters) are simply prepared but incredibly fresh. No reservations.

Lupa (170 Thompson St, tel: 212-982-5089, map D2) is one of celebrity chef Mario Batali's first NYC restaurants and is still a standout for its delicious rustic Italian fare and decor, great wine list and fun but noisy atmosphere. Lunch is a quieter experience.

Aki (181 W. 4th St, tel: 212-989-5440, map C3) is a hidden gem for sushi-lovers. The chef spent a few years working for the Japanese ambassador to Jamaica, and his top-notch creations are tinged with Caribbean flavours. It's tiny here, so be sure to reserve in advance.

For one of the best falafels or Mediterranean platters (hummus, pita, cucumber salad) join the line-up at **Taim** (222 Waverly Place). Seating is limited, but you can always head a few blocks east to Washington Square and enjoy a picnic there (*see p.105*).

Soho, Tribeca, and Chinatown

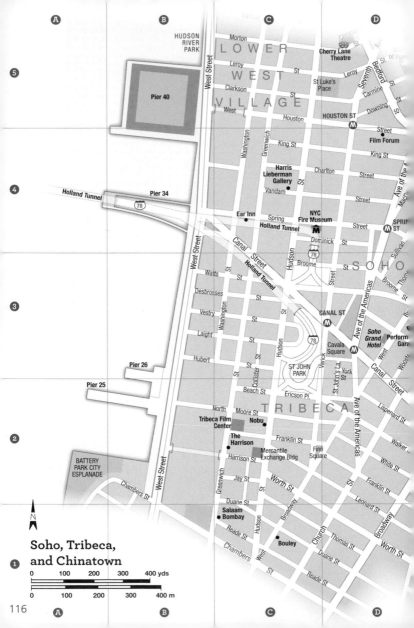

Soho, Tribeca,
and Chinatown

Dig into steaming **dim sum in Chinatown**

New York's Chinatown is one of the largest Chinese enclaves in the world outside of Asia, and that means there's a huge choice of places to eat. But not all are good – New York foodies have a shortlist of the places they like to go to:

Take a steep escalator ride up to **Jing Fong** (18 Elizabeth St, tel: 212-964-5256, map F1), a huge, bustling banquet hall crowded with patrons who choose from a wide variety of Hong Kong-style dim sum passing by their tables on rolling carts. It's best to go closer to 10am when the food is freshest. They close at 3.30pm.

There are no rolling carts at **Dim Sum Go-Go** (5 East Broadway, tel: 212-732-0796, map F1), with its easy-to-order, reasonably priced dim sum menu – 24 kinds on offer. Recommended are the dim sum

platter (good for the dim sum novice) and the roast chicken with fried garlic stems.

There's usually a line-up to get into **Joe's Shanghai** (9 Pell St, tel: 212-233-8888, map F1) to order their famous mouthwatering soup dumplings filled with pork or crabmeat. Other dishes are good here too, like the Szechuan string beans, salt-and-pepper prawns with shells, and the Shanghai noodles.

Oriental Garden (14 Elizabeth St, tel: 212-619-0085, map F1) attracts big-name chefs like Daniel Bouley, who come here for the exceptionally fresh seafood. It can be noisy and the menu can vary in quality. But you can't go wrong ordering seafood dishes like the fried shrimp balls, lobster in XO sauce, or oysters with shiitake mushrooms and scallions.

Shop for **designer knockoffs** on **Canal Street**

The heart of Chinatown, Canal Street is hectic with pedestrian traffic and vociferous street vendors. It has long been the place to go for counterfeit designer products, but a police crackdown has cut down on the number of knockoff handbags, watches, jewelry, and shades displayed in the open on this crowded street. Customers are not at risk of arrest, but vendors are. Still, it hasn't dissuaded intrepid salespeople from reaching out to tourists who crowd the street in the afternoons and on weekends – they've simply become more stealthy.

If you're looking for a fake designer accessory, watch for men on street corners with wallet-size plastic catalogues of product photos. Then, either they'll lead you down the back stairwell of a store, or around a corner to another address. What happens afterwards is not for the faint of heart: you'll be taken into rooms that may then be locked behind you. Spread out on the floor will be a selection of faux brand-name accoutrements to choose from – Gucci, Cartier, Prada – you name it, there's a fake for it.

Alternatively, locate one of the minivans parked just off Canal Street, used by mobile vendors who are ready to move on at the slightest sign of police activity.

Canal Street, Chinatown; map F1

HOW TO SHOP FOR A FAKE

• Don't be afraid to haggle, especially if you're buying more than one item
• Do your research on the latest trends before you buy if you don't want an out-of-date fake
• If you don't see what you want, ask. Chances are someone will have it 'in stock'.
• Be sure to look carefully at the items, and look for shoddy workmanship like zippers that don't close, or seams that aren't sewn together correctly.
• Remember to carry cash, but not too much, as visible wads won't help in your negotiations
• Avoid buying pirated DVDs – usually shot by home video cameras in theaters and terrible quality.

Catch a foreign film at **Film Forum**, then raise a pint at **the historic Ear Inn**

A cinephile's paradise, **The Film Forum** has been New York's leading movie house for indie premieres, classic and foreign films, and director retrospectives since 1970 when it began with 50 folding chairs and one screen. On any given week you could, for example, catch an original Godzilla movie, see part of a Robert Altman retrospective, watch a restored print of Jean-Luc Godard's *Breathless*, or attend a premiere of the latest documentary by D. A. Pennebaker *(Don't Look Back)* with the director on hand for questions after the screening.

People complain the three screens in the theatre are small and the seats uncomfortable, but film-lovers agree it just wouldn't be the same in the city without the Film Forum's eclectic and well-thought-out screening programs.

A great place for a drink or bar meal (burgers, steak and fries) afterwards is the historic **Ear Inn**. Built in 1817 by the water's edge to serve thirsty longshoremen working the docks, it's been called the Ear Inn since the 1970s, after the 'B' in the neon 'Bar' sign was transformed with a few dabs of paint into an 'E' by members of *The Ear* music magazine, then published on the premises. Thanks to landfill and development, the former speakeasy now sits a few blocks inland. It has become a city institution where people come to enjoy a drink or meal in a relaxed atmosphere and maybe catch some live jazz if it's a music night.

The Film Forum, 209 W. Houston St; www.filmforum.org; map D4
The Ear Inn, 326 Spring St; tel: 212-226-9060; map C4

Take in the sight and smell of 280,000 pounds of topsoil at the **New York Earth Room**

You push a buzzer at a nondescript door in Soho tucked between high-end furniture and clothing boutiques, and head up a flight of stairs to what is perhaps the longest-running and most unusual free art display in the city, the New York Earth Room.

It's a sprawling 22-inch pile of dark, humid topsoil filling a 3,600-square-foot loft the size of a small football field. The same earth has been sitting here for nearly 35 years, the work of artist Walter De Maria, one of three Earth Rooms he has created since 1968, and the only one still in existence.

The exhibit is maintained and run by the Dia Art Foundation, a not-for-profit arts organization that likes to support artworks that wouldn't otherwise be able to exist. Not only is this one of the longest-running art exhibits in the city, but the person who mans the exhibit has perhaps one of New York's longest-running jobs. For more than 20 years he has greeted the public and tended the soil, raking and watering it weekly, occasionally finding small weeds or mushrooms growing which he carefully removes.

About 50 people come here a day, and reaction to the show is diverse. Some New Yorkers say it's the most soil they've seen in years, some find it mildly creepy, others say being here is spiritual or comforting, a moment of peace in the hectic city. Many are drawn back to the room again and again.

You can't photograph it, or touch it, but you can ask questions, like how they got the soil in here in the first place (through the windows with cranes) or what it means (that's up to you).

The New York Earth Room, 141 Wooster St; www.earthroom.org; Wed–Sun, noon–6pm (closed 3–3.30pm), closed from mid-June to mid-Sept; free; map E4

Buy a hip messenger bag, an antique human skull, or a first-edition photo on **a Soho shopping spree**

It's hard to find a higher-quality or more picturesque shopping district than Soho. The cobblestone streets are lined with beautiful and spacious cast-iron buildings, and their high-ceilinged stores sell some of the best designs in clothes, furniture, and household goods you'll find in North America. Stroll around and you're certain to stumble on something that will give you inspiration. Here's a tour that takes you to some of the more interesting shops in the area.

Check out some of the best in industrial and decorative design at **Moss** (150 Greene St, map E4), its 7,000 square feet of curated furniture, watches, dishware, jewelry, and more blurring the line between museum and shop. If you're in the mood for some luxury lingerie, satin sheets, corsets, or gold-plated handcuffs, head to **Kiki de Montparnasse** (79 Greene St, map E3). The change rooms have three choices of lighting: before, during, and after.

Purl Patchwork (459 Broome St, map E3) has a great selection of beautiful fabrics ranging from Japanese and French imports to reproductions of Victorian-era designs. **Swiss Army** (136 Prince St, map E4) has more than just knives. There are also great watches, luggage, and clothes. You can see or buy the very best in music photography of the last half-century at **Morrison Hotel Gallery** (124 Prince St, map E4), which also has great temporary exhibits. The **Apple Store** (103 Prince St, map E4) is New York's flagship store and holds hourly free presentations in the auditorium on anything you need to know about Apple products.

For great outdoor apparel and gear for hiking and climbing head to **Patagonia** (101 Wooster St, map E3). Charming **Betsy Johnson** (138 Wooster St, map E4) burst onto the scene in the 1980s, and still entertains us with her beautiful, fun, and flirty frocks. For those drawn to more morbid subjects, there's

Evolution (120 Spring St, map E3). Buy framed butterflies or insects, a stuffed rat, or a human skull for $895 at this quirky store selling natural history collectables.

MoMA Design Store (81 Spring St, map E3) presents two floors of carefully chosen products ranging from chairs to notebooks, scarves, and watches by classic and new designers. Great for gift shopping.

Kate's Paperie (72 Spring St, map F3) has a great selection of gorgeous paper, stationery, cards, and writing supplies, while **Prada** (575 Broadway, map F3) is worth visiting for the sensational Rem Koolhas-designed interior.

Honor the kid in you or in your life at the **Scholastic Store** (557 Broadway, map E3). This enormous retail space sells thousands of high-quality and educational children's books and toys. A little further along, find inexpensive stylish clothes at the world flagship store of **Uniqlo** (546 Broadway, map E3) – think H&M with a Japanese minimalist twist.

Finally **Kate Spade** (454 Broome St, map E3) is a new American classic handbag, luggage, clothing, and shoe designer with a slightly quirky and retro feel. For great men's bags and clothes try **Jack Spade** (56 Greene St, map E3).

Take in the beauty of **cast-iron architecture** at its most splendid in Soho

A new type of building construction appeared in New York in the mid-late 1800s that would become the precursor to the skyscraper: the use of prefabricated cast iron for building facades and interior support columns. The relatively inexpensive cast iron could be molded into intricate designs and patterns for the facades, while the strength of the metal allowed for higher ceilings and taller windows, permitting more natural light to flow into industrial buildings and warehouses in this pre-electrical era. The low-cost iron was an easy and inexpensive way to add decoration to utilitarian commercial buildings. More than 250 of these buildings exist in New York and most of them are in Soho. Here are a few worth seeking out:

At the northeast corner of Broadway and Broome is the **E. V. Haughwout Building** (*pictured*, map E3), one of the first cast-iron structures in the city which took just one year to build. When unveiled in 1857, it boasted the world's first hydraulic passenger elevator.

Dating from 1873, the **Gunther Building** at the southwest corner of Broome and Greene boasts an elegant Second Empire facade, a style popular in the 1870s, with regularly spaced Corinthian columns and ornate cornices, balustrades, and brackets.

Damage to **71 Greene Street** on the first and second stories of the building reveals how the ornamental cast-iron plates were bolted onto the facade. The ornate three-dimensional facade of **72 Greene Street** is considered the area's finest example of cast-iron splendor. The facade at **10 Greene Street**, built in 1869, has heavy, unadorned Tuscan columns. Like other buildings in the area, it is partly obscured by fire escapes – a legal requirement after a series of loft fires swept the city in 1915.

Greene Street; map E3

Devour homemade **Chinese ice cream** and observe community life in Chinatown's **Columbus Park**

On warm-weather days, the line can get long at the **Chinatown Ice Cream Factory**, but the delectable scoops of ice cream made on the premises are well worth the wait. Open since 1978, this little ice-cream parlor has spawned a number of competitors, but there's no disputing that the original is the best. The ice creams and sorbets come in traditional flavors like chocolate, coffee, rocky road, or pistachio. But there's also an enticing choice of exotic Asian flavors to tingle your taste buds, such as ginger, green tea, lychee, or black sesame.

The best place to enjoy your ice cream is nearby **Columbus Park**, the de facto community center of bustling Chinatown. Some say it resembles a square in China 70 years ago: along the fences and under canopies cobblers, fortune-tellers, jewelry repairers, and booksellers ply their trade. Inside the park, Chinese men and women play tile games, dominoes, and mahjong, some gambling and smoking. Others practice martial arts and Tai Chi while families stroll by or young lovers sit on benches. A frequent sight on weekends is a group of seniors playing traditional Chinese instruments, accompanied on occasion by retired Cantonese opera singers. Boxed in by skyscrapers lining Baxter, Worth, Bayard and Mulberry streets, the park was recently refurbished with new plantings and landscaping and is a welcome place of relaxation.

Chinatown Ice Cream Factory, 65 Bayard St, weekends only, 11am–11pm, weather depending; map E1
Columbus Park, 67 Mulberry St; map E1

Join the power-breakfast set at **Balthazar** or sip tea in the exclusive **Mercer Hotel lounge**

Rather than jostle with the evening crowds, a weekday breakfast at **Balthazar** is a great way to experience this Soho institution. The breakfast here is not overly pricey, and both the food and the company are worthy of note – Balthazar in the morning has become an unofficial meeting and deal-making spot for writers, editors, and new media tycoons who work nearby – *The Huffington Post*'s New York headquarters are around the corner, as is the head office of Gawker.com. Balthazar bakery is next door, so the bread basket is a heavenly assortment of freshly baked rolls, raisin bread, and slices of fresh whole wheat and rye, ideal for dipping in soft-boiled eggs cooked to perfection.

Or, dig into fresh croissants, eggs benedict, or a creamy quiche.

For more celebrity-spotting, or to feel like one yourself, enjoy a glass of wine or cup of tea in the Christian Liagre-designed lounge of the nearby **Mercer Hotel**. It's really only meant for guests, but if you're well-dressed and discreet, no one will mind you sitting a while on one of the leather banquettes or inviting armchairs and soaking up the sophisticated library-like atmosphere. Keep your eyes peeled for high-profile models, directors and actors who stay here, and are often interviewed in the lounge.

Balthazar, 80 Spring St; tel: 212-925-5340; map E3
Mercer Hotel, 141 Mercer St; tel: 212-965-3800; map E4

Pick up some **ginseng, Chinese slippers**, or hard-to-find **Asian food**

The axis of Chinatown is slowly shifting to less expensive Flushing in the borough of Queens, and many longtime businesses didn't survive the severe economic fallout of 9/11 (the World Trade Center was not far away). But the area still bustles with businesses catering to Chinese and tourists alike. Here are a few places to shop for Asian food, household goods, and knick-knacks.

Hong Kong Supermarket is the largest Asian supermarket in Manhattan. Upstairs you'll find a wide selection of sauces, beverages from all over Asia, and frozen dumplings. Downstairs, the aisles are lined with snacks, dried goods, herbs, and a small selection of bowls, woks, and steamers. It helps to speak Cantonese, and it can get extremely crowded on weekends when management gives out free food samples. Some complain the ringing-up process at checkout is often dodgy, so pay attention as prices are keyed in.

Be prepared to spend a couple of hours at **Pearl River Mart**, a treasure trove of Asian bargains. You'll find everything from birdcages and glittery satin jackets to 200 types of lacquered chopsticks, sushi dishes, Chinese slippers, window shades, insulated lunch-bags, and low-priced comestibles like sushi rice, rice vinegar, or soy sauce. It is clean and well organized, with goods spread out over three levels. The soothing sounds of Chinese Musak will lull you into a state of shopping bliss. Perfect for unusual gifts.

Kam Man Food Products is a bustling food and home goods store that's a fun place to roam. It's great for Asian sauces and candy, as well as cookware, dishes, and chopsticks.

Hong Kong Supermarket, 68 Elizabeth St; tel: 212-966-4943; map F2
Pearl River Mart, 477 Broadway; tel: 212-431-4770; map E3
Kam Man Food Products, 200 Canal St; tel: 212-571-0330; map F1

Eat with the Elite in **Tribeca**

Once a dark and desolate corner of the city, Tribeca today is home to wealthy young families who enjoy high-end loft living. Foodies make the trek to this revitalized area for some of the best restaurants in the city.

At the top of the list is **Bouley** (163 Duane St, tel: 212-964-2525, map C1). Big windows onto the street reveal the kitchen where you might spot celebrity chef David Bouley at work. Inside, patrons enjoy haute cuisine in a refined romantic atmosphere. Dig into the five-course tasting meal, or order dishes like the Cape Cod baby squid with scallops and crabmeat, and remember, high quality doesn't come cheap.

You might find yourself next to Nicole Kidman, P. Diddy, or Robert DeNiro at crowded **Nobu** (*pictured*, 105 Hudson St; tel: 212-219-0500, map C2), which De Niro helped launch with chef Nobu Matsuhisa more than a decade ago. Patrons are wowed by his nouvelle haute Japanese cuisine: a house favorite is broiled black cod with miso, and the sushi and hand rolls are consistently excellent. The $150 tasting menu is a good way to discover why it's so hard to get a seat here. You might have more luck at the simpler and cozier Nobu Nextdoor, next door.

The Harrison (355 Greenwich St, tel: 212-274-9310, map C2) serves a new American menu (horseradish-encrusted salmon, duck-fat fries) in a cozy and classy space with dim lighting and excellent bartenders that's made it a low-key Tribeca favorite. Enjoy the outdoor seating in warm weather.

For Euro-glamor and the best Bellini in town, head just north of Tribeca to **Cipriani Downtown** (376 W. Broadway, tel: 212-343-0999; map E3), perfect for spotting models and celebrities. The food isn't bad either: try the octopus carpaccio, the lobster salad, or the freshly made ravioli.

Discover the works of well-known and emerging artists at Soho's **intimate art galleries**

In the late 1970s and '80s the Soho gallery scene was in full swing, when exhibits by artists like Keith Haring and Jean-Michel Basquiat attracted hordes of black-clad hipsters and well-heeled collectors. But as boutiques and restaurants mushroomed, galleries closed or moved, and artists sought pastures new. By 2000 Chelsea had become the center of the gallery scene *(see p.83)*. However, a surprising number of important galleries still remain in Soho, here's a selection of places worth exploring for temporary exhibits and their permanent collections:

Ronald Feldman Fine Arts Gallery (31 Mercer St, tel: 212-226-3232, map E2). Serious conceptual art by museum-quality artists.

Martin Lawrence Galleries (457 West Broadway, tel: 212-995-8865, map E4). Well-known and emerging artists: paintings, sculpture, and graphic design.

Franklin Bowles Galleries (431 West Broadway, tel: 212-226-1616, map E4). A 'Blue Chip' gallery featuring valuable works by Chagall, Dalí, Miró and more.

Louis K. Meisel Gallery (141 Prince St, tel: 212-677-1340, map E4). Owns the largest pin-up art collection in the world.

June Kelly Gallery (166 Mercer St, tel: 212-226-1660, map F4). Contemporary works by African-American artists.

Clic Gallery and Bookstore (424 Broome St, tel: 212-219-9308, map E3). Monthly shows by emerging photographers, and a curated selection of high-quality photography books *(pictured)*.

Margarete Roeder Gallery (545 Broadway, 4th Floor, tel: 212-925-6098, map E3). Specializes in drawings by Merce Cunningham, and contemporary German prints.

Harris Lieberman Gallery (89 Vandam St, tel: 212-206-1290, map C4). Important young art gallery presenting new artists. Off the beaten path in both its location and curating.

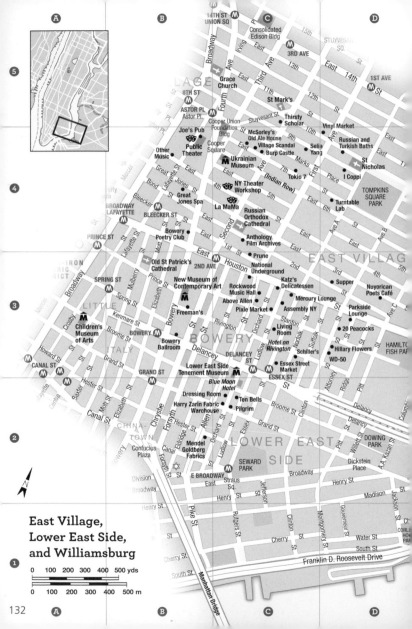

East Village,
Lower East Side,
and Williamsburg

0   100 200 300 400 500 yds

0   100 200 300 400 500 m

Buy a hipster hat or handmade jewelry at a **one-of-a-kind boutique**

In your wanderings through the streets of the East Village and Lower East Side you'll stumble across many interesting boutiques selling an assortment of individual items, from handmade jewelry and vintage rock T-shirts to trendy sneakers and wedding dresses.

For a fun hat-shopping experience, try **Village Scandal** (19 E. 7th St, map C4) in the East Village, which sells everything from hipster hats to panamas and their own custom cloche. For the latest in DJ turntables and a good choice of vinyl, head to the **Turntable Lab** (120 E. 7th St, map D4; *see page 144 for more places to buy old LPS and CDs in the area*).

Vintage clothes stores and one-of-a-kind clothing boutiques line East 9th Street between Avenue A and second Avenue. Head for resale/consignment shop **Tokio 7** (83 E. 7th St, map C4) and poke

through great designer duds. Getting married? You'll find gorgeous bridal gowns at **Selia Yang** (328 E. 9th St, map C4).

On the Lower East Side a number of designer co-op boutiques have sprung up, which showcase the work of emerging designers. Singer-songwriter **Hillary Flowers** also runs a boutique (40 Clinton St, map D3) featuring the work of about 20 designers, whose goods are put on display in exchange for working in the store. **The Dressing Room** (75a Orchard St, map C2) is both bar and hip designer emporium, with used and vintage clothes downstairs. **Pilgrim** (70 Orchard St, map C2) is a boutique owned by designers with Donna Karan and Anna Sui, who show off their own affordable designs here. **Pixie Market** (100 Stanton St, map C3) showcases international up-and-coming designers.

For men, **20 Peacocks** (20 Clinton St, map D3) sells high-end European-style men's shirts and ties. The *New York Times* calls nearby **Assembly New York** (174 Ludlow St, map C3) 'the best curated men's wear store in the city.' Alongside its own designs it stocks an imaginative selection of other brands and vintage apparel.

Observe human and animal life at **Tompkins Square Park**, then hear some **Western swing**

Tompkins Square Park has been a symbol of social unrest and alternative lifestyles since it opened in 1850 – it was reportedly remodeled in 1936 better to divide and manage crowds that gathered here to protest. The park was an infamous gathering place for hippies and runaways in the 1960s. By the 1980s it was a no-go zone of violent crime and drug-dealing, and became a focal point for conflicts between homeless activists and police. Attempts to oust them in 1988 sparked a two-day riot. With the area's gradual gentrification, today's Tompkins Square Park is an altogether more peaceful place: young professionals, families, students, and seniors come here to sit on park benches, enjoy arts festivals, or play on the basketball courts or playgrounds.

One of the main draws of the park is the large **dog run**, complete with bathing areas, where apartment-bound dogs of all breeds and sizes are let off the leash by their owners to scamp around and maybe get a hose down. Look up and take in the rare sight of dozens of **American Elms**, among the few elm trees in the country not wiped out by Dutch Elm disease.

Every year around Labor Day, crowds pack the park for the **Howl! Arts Festival** inspired by former East Village resident Allen Ginsberg's epic poem. The highlight is the drag queen festival **Wigstock**. The weekend before, the park celebrates another former resident with the **Charlie Parker Jazz Festival**: two days of free concerts. Park goers also enjoy **classic French films** at sunset each Friday night in June and July.

For some fun bluegrass, country or Western swing, and cheap beer, neighborhood nightspot **Banjo Jim's** is worth knowing about.

Tompkins Square Park; map D4
Banjo Jim's, 700 E. 9th St; tel: 212-777-0869; map E4

Bite into an **authentic pastrami sandwich**, then go hear some **American roots music**

Katz's Delicatessen (205 E. Houston St, map C3) is one of the last big delis on the Lower East Side, packing in locals, tourists, and people heading to hear music in the area which is full of great little venues. Katz's has what some say is the best pastrami sandwich in the city, with the meat sliced by hand, and served with giant homemade pickles. Place your order at the counter, then jostle for a seat at a table. You might end up occupying the very seat in which Meg Ryan played out her famous 'climax' scene in *When Harry Met Sally*. Cash only.

Nora Jones honed her craft a couple of blocks away at the mellow **Living Room** (154 Ludlow St, map C3), which features several good bands a night with no cover charge. **Arlene's Grocery** (95 Stanton St, map C3) showcases new rock, metal, and indie bands for a cheap cover. Bluegrass, alt-country, and American roots are the focus at the intimate **Rockwood Music Hall** (196 Allen St, map C3), or at the louder two-level **National Underground** (159 E. Houston St, map C3). On Monday nights the **Parkside Lounge** (317 E. Houston St, map D3) hosts great bluegrass jams. Good indie and alternative bands play **The Mercury Lounge** (217 E. Houston St, map C3) and even better bands from around the world play the historic **Bowery Ballroom** (6 Delancey St, map B3).

Raise a pint at a **historic tavern**

Open since the mid-1850s, **McSorley's Old Ale House** is the oldest Irish tavern in the city, and it feels like it with its sawdust floor, worn wood doors, and walls covered with yellowing newspaper clippings and artwork including a wanted poster for Lincoln's assassin. Everyone from Teddy Roosevelt to John Lennon has been here at some point, and it still packs in a crowd. Drinking here doesn't require much thought: there are just two types of ale, light and dark, that come in little half-pint mugs for $4.50.

A few doors down, the worship of beer continues at **Burp Castle** with its quirky medieval-style murals, piped Gregorian chant, and bartenders occasionally dressed as monks. There are 12 types of draft beer and 40 brands

of potent bottled beer imported from Belgium, Germany, and Britain. Free French fries from the nearby Belgian Pommes Frites shop are passed out from 5.30pm until supplies run out. Heavenly.

At the **Thirsty Scholar** around the corner, there's no evidence that the wild-haired effigy of Mark Twain, the piles of musty books, or the beady-eyed portrait of Samuel Beckett inspire intellectual debate. Most serious thought given by locals at this cozy, low-ceilinged pub is on what to drink.

McSorley's Old Ale House, 15 E. 7th St; tel: 212-474-9148; map C4
Burp Castle, 41 E. 7th St; tel: 212-982-4576; map C4
Thirsty Scholar, 155 Second Ave; tel: 212-777-6514; map C5

Drink or dine in a cool **Lower East Side bar or restaurant**

Foodies looking for adventure off the beaten path head to the Lower East Side, where small eateries pack them in thanks to interesting menus and a hip but mature vibe.

LOWER EAST SIDE

The intersection of Broome and Orchard streets is one of the more fashionable in the area. **Little Giant** (85 Orchard St, tel: 212-226-5027, map C2) is a hip yet homey spot serving fresh, organic and imaginative seasonal dishes like scallops with hazelnuts and pulled Berkshire pork on a butternut

scone. Just around the corner the hot new downtown wine bar, **Ten Bells** (247 Broome St, tel: 212-228-4450, map C2) serves organic wine by the glass or the bottle accompanied by yummy nibbles – rillettes, mixed cheese plates, fresh oysters – in a dimly lit, cozily rustic space. Fashionable **Freeman's** (8 Rivington St, end of Freeman's Alley, tel: 212-420-0012, map B3) a pioneer of the hunting-lodge chic look, serves sophisticated American traditional food (wild-boar terrine, summer pudding). Meatballs have made a comeback

in Manhattan, witnessed by the popular **Meatball Shop** (84 Stanton St, tel: 212-982-8895, map C3), which has a wide-ranging meatball menu from classic beef, chicken, or spicy pork to salmon or vegetarian.

Serious foodies head to **WD-50** (50 Clinton St, tel: 212-477-2900, map D3) where chef Willie Dufresne invents wildly imaginative concoctions like foie gras with passion fruit puree and beer ice cream. **Schiller's Liquor Bar** (131 Rivington St, tel: 212-260-4555, map C3) is a bohemian bar and bistro, serving the fashionable,

the local and the suited. For pancakes, pies and freshly baked goods, head to **The Clinton St. Baking Company** (4 Clinton St, tel: 646-602-6263, map D3) – a popular brunch and lunch spot.

For some people-watching and the wow-factor, have a drink in the dramatic lounge of the **Hotel on Rivington** (107 Rivington St, map C3); or try to get past the velvet ropes at the exclusive penthouse bar **Above Allen** (190 Allen St, map C3) with its sensational view of the New York skyline. A scruffy but fun alternative, lively dive bar **Max Fish** (178 Ludlow St, map C3) lays on cheap beer, a pool table and a great jukebox.

EAST VILLAGE

A few blocks north in the East Village, **Supper** (156 E. 2nd St, tel: 212-477-7600, map D3) is a current downtown favorite, serving rustic Italian in a crowded yet convivial space. **Prune** (54 E. 1st St, tel: 212-677-6221, map C3) has a polished menu of American dishes with ethnic twists, and a great weekend brunch. Delicious smells waft from the wood-burning oven into **I Coppi** (432 E. 9th St, tel: 212-254-2263, map D4), a relaxed but sophisticated Tuscan restaurant with a great outdoor garden.

Go on a whirlwind **hipster tour of Williamsburg**, Brooklyn

Start by having brunch or a mimosa at magnificent, old-world **Dressler** (149 Broadway, map G1), or try simple and delicious French fare at cozy **Le Barricou** (553 Grand St, tel: 718-782-7372, map H2).

Then head out to Bedford Avenue, the area's main shopping drag, chockablock with clothing and antique shops, cafes, and restaurants. Start at **Brooklyn Industries** (no. 162), where messenger bags and cool T's for both men and women are hot items, or poke through the well-edited selection of emerging women's wear designers (Steve Allen, Rag & Bone) at **Jumelle** (no. 148). One of the more interesting vintage clothes stores on Bedford is **Mini Mini Market** (no. 218), a tiny, funky shop crammed with clothes, great shoes and bags, and locally made jewelry. Get some vintage CDs and LPS at **Earwax** next door, or browse the crammed bookshelves at quirky **Spoonbill and Sugartown** a few doors down, then head next door to **Verb Café** to study hipsters in their natural environment. If you're craving a snack, get a free cheese sample at the **Bedford Gourmet Cheese Shop** (no. 229).

When you're ready for dinner, try the cozy and packed **Diner** (85 Broadway, tel: 718-486-3077), a favorite with celebrity chef Anthony Bourdain for its grass-fed burger and organic new American cuisine. If the wait is too long, go next door to **Marlow & Sons** (81 Broadway, tel: 718-384-1441), owned by the same family and famous for its oysters, great wine selection and hospitable, slightly upscale atmosphere. Then it's time for what Brooklyn is really famous for these days: music (see page 147).

Bedford Avenue; map H2

Chill out in an old-school **Russian bath** or **New Age spa**

For nigh-on 100 years, East Villagers have been unwinding at the **Russian and Turkish baths**, an old-school and slightly worse-for-wear bathhouse where, once you've donned the requisite robe and sandals, you are well advised to attach yourself to the garrulous regulars and follow their established ritual. This includes a bake in a Russian sauna, a *shvitz* in a Turkish bath filled with clouds of lavender-scented steam, and frequent plunges into the ice-cold pool. For a small extra fee, attendants will flagellate you with oak leaves soaked in olive oil, scrub you in Dead Sea salts, and cake you in mud. A session ends with a cup of borscht or plate of chopped herring in the on-premises **Anna's Restaurant**. You can find plenty of fancier places in New York to soak and sweat, but the cracked tiles and chatter infused with old-world lilts provide an only-in-New-York ambience that's as refreshing as the treatment.

The nearby **Great Jones Spa** puts a New Age spin on tried-and-true bathhouse standards in a Water Lounge filled with all sorts of fancy wizardry, including a steam room aglow with health-inducing chakra lights.

Russian and Turkish Baths, 368 E. 10th St; tel: 212-674-9250; www.russianturkbaths.com; map D4
Great Jones Spa, 29 Great Jones St; tel: 212-505-3185; www.greatjonesspa.com; map B4

Celebrate the spirit of Allen Ginsberg at a **poetry reading**, then peek at **cutting-edge filmmaking**

Beat poet Allen Ginsberg's presence is alive in the East Village at the **Nuyorican Poets Café**, which Ginsberg called 'the most integrated place on the planet' because of its mix of white, Afro-Cuban, and African-American rappers and poets, musicians and storytellers, performing in many languages. This cultural institution maintains its long-standing street cred in its current home, a high-ceilinged, brick-walled space on East 3rd Street in Alphabet City. Crowds line up around the block to cram into the small club for the Friday night poetry slam, but also worth checking out is the hip-hop poetry and jazz open jam, Afro-Cuban jazz evenings, or the open-mic prison-writing night called *Write from Wrong*.

Spoken-word junkies will also love the **Bowery Poetry Club**, which bills itself a 'playground for language.' This spacious cafe with a party atmosphere puts on about 20-30 shows a week, hosting poetry slams and readings, burlesque and jazz with poetry, and monthly events like poetry and stories from Andy Warhol alum Taylor Mead, and the Urbana Thunderslam open-mic poetry slam.

Cinephiles will find paradise at **The Anthology Film Archives**, devoted to archiving, restoring, and showing the best in experimental film. Programmers dig into the vault and show several screenings a day of classic and cutting-edge documentaries and art films, along with filmmaker retrospectives and premieres. The seats are uncomfortable, it can be hot in the summer and cold in the winter, the roof is known to leak, but hardcore film buffs don't complain.

Nuyorican Poets Café, 236 E. 3rd St; tel: 212-505-8183; www.nuyorikan.org; map D3
The Bowery Poetry Club, 308 Bowery; tel: 212-614-0505; www.bowerypoetry. com; map B4
The Anthology Film Archives, 32 Second Ave; tel: 212-505-5181; www. anthologyfilmarchives.org; map C4

Eat a curry on **Indian Row**

Christmas lights – are so similar there's an urban myth they share the same block-long underground kitchen. There are two standouts: **Brick Lane Curry House** (306 East 6th St, tel: 212-979 2900) has a light, airy decor and a menu a notch above the others. Indian foodies praise their garlic naan and the Goan curry, the house specialty. Just around the corner is **Banjara** (91 First Ave, tel: 212-477-5956), where the popular dish is Lamb Dumpakht, a buttery chicken or lamb curry cooked in pastry like a giant dumpling. Great people-watching from the front windows.

On 6th Street between Second and First Avenues is **Indian Row**, where about a dozen Indian food restaurants compete for customers. Their menus and decor – heavy on all-year-round

Indian Row, on 6th St, between Second and First aves; map C4

LITTLE INDIA

The official Little India in Manhattan is a several-block radius of Indian eateries and shops centered on Lexington Avenue near 26th Street (another Little India is in Jackson Heights, Queens). A standout choice here is **Pongal** (110 Lexington Street, tel: 212-696-9458, map p.79 F3), across from the famous food and spice shops **Foods of India** and **Kalustyan's**. Pongal serves authentic vegetarian South Indian fare; recommended are the delicious *dosas* and the Royal Thali.

At **Vatan** (409 Third Ave at 29th St, tel: 212-689-5666 map p.79 G3) you take off your shoes and sit on cushions in a decor evocative of a village in Gujarat. Waitresses serve generous helpings of tasty vegetarian thali in pre-set menus.

Some Indian food fans say the best in the city is at **Salaam Bombay** in Tribeca (319 Greenwich St, tel: 212-226-9400, map p.116 C1), though there are complaints about poor service.

For upscale, inspired New Indian dishes that get rave reviews, head to **Tabla** (11 Madison Ave, tel: 212-889-0667, map p.79 E3) in the Flatiron District.

Rub shoulders with DJs while shopping for **turntables, LPs, and CDs** in the East Village

Record and CD collectors, and DJ wannabes head for the East Village, an area with a history of setting music trends. Its heyday was in the 1970s–90s when many now-legendary bands paid their dues here like Luscious Jackson, Talking Heads, Dee-Lite, Patti Smith, and the Ramones to name but a few. High rents have pushed the indie-rock and roots-music scene to Brooklyn *(see p.147)*, and music clubs are now centered on the Lower East Side *(see p.136)*, but the East Village is clinging with tenacity to its musical past as the destination for DJs, and LP and CD collectors.

At **Other Music** (15 E. 4th St, map B4), DJs and musicians flip through carefully curated rare and experimental records. Helpful blurbs are posted on new indie-rock arrivals, and there's a great selection of quirkier finds from obscure psychedelia to Polynesian electronica. **Turntable Lab** (120 E. 7th St, map D4) is a one-stop source for both aspiring and professional DJs, selling basic equipment and high-tech add-ons, as well as a small but eclectic vinyl collection. At **Vinyl Market** (241 E. 10th St, D4), well-known Japanese DJ Kaz Okura sells pure electronica. **Good Records** (218 E. 5th St, map C4) has carefully chosen rock, soul, jazz, hip-hop, funk and reggae vinyl. **Gimme Gimme Records** (325 E. 5th St, map C4) carries a good selection of disco, house and techno vinyl, but is only open Fri–Sun 1–10pm.

To watch DJs in action any time of day or night, pass by the street-level studio of the internet radio station **East Village Radio**. Up to 60 DJs take turns playing excellent and rare music in a mix of genres in two-hour blocks.

Shop for imported **high-end fabrics at low prices**

Rising rents and encroaching gentrification have forced many of Manhattan's neighborhood haberdashers and fabric merchants out of business, as their premises are snapped up by trendy boutiques and bars. But there are a few survivors in the Lower East Side, which remains a good destination for excellent, keenly priced furnishing textiles.

For the best selection of upholstery and drapery fabric in the city, head to **Harry Zarin Fabric Warehouse**. The cavernous building is filled with fabric and notions. They buy directly from mills and manufacturers, so can offer steep discounts on luxurious designer fabrics. The company is known for supplying set designers on major TV shows shooting in the New York area, including *30 Rock*, *Law & Order*, and *Sex and the City*.

An equally impressive array of domestic and imported fabrics and trimmings can be found at **Joe's Fabric Warehouse**.

The Fashion District has the best choice of apparel fabric shops (*see box*), but there are a couple of noteworthy outlets round here: **Mendel Goldberg Fabrics**, which also sells quilting and needlepoint supplies, and **Belraf Fabrics**, a narrow shop with a wide selection.

Harry Zarin Fabric Warehouse, 314 Grand St; tel: 212-925-6112; map C2

Joe's Fabric Warehouse, 102 Orchard St; tel: 212-674-7089; map C3

Mendel Goldberg Fabrics, 72 Hester St; tel: 212-925-9110; map B2

Belraf Fabrics, 159 Orchard St; tel: 212-505-2106; map C3

MIDTOWN FABRIC SHOPS

While the East Village is known for upholstery fabric, the best selection of outlets for clothing fabric is in the Midtown Fashion District. At **Mood** (225 W. 37th St, map p.58 C2), professionals and amateur seamstresses spend hours poking through the huge and well-priced fabric selection.

Made famous by the hit TV series *Project Runway*, **B&J Fabrics** (525 Seventh Ave, map p.58 C2) stocks only beautiful, quality fabrics and is slightly pricier. The best selection of buttons and trimmings in the city is at **M&J Trimming** (1008 Sixth Ave, map p.58 D1).

Step into a **19th-century time capsule** and marvel at America's first **synagogue**

Families who sought a new life in the United States during the great era of immigration (1880–1920), often found their first American home in a building such as the gaunt six-story brick tenement on the Lower East Side which now houses the **Tenement Museum**. Over a span of seven decades, this one building was home to more than 7,000 people from some 20 countries. In 1935, the upstairs apartments were sealed by the landlord, who didn't want to bring them to code. On the discovery of this inadvertent time capsule, more than half a century later, the building was converted into a museum. One flat has been left exactly as it was found when the building was reopened, while others have been recreated to provide insight into the families' ethnic backgrounds and daily lives. Tour guides tell compelling stories about the people who lived there and the resilience with which they sought to combat poverty and assimilate into New York life.

A visit to the nearby **Eldridge Street Synagogue**, restored to its former glory after a 20-year restoration, will shed further light on the lives of immigrants, for whom religion played such an important role. Both places can only be seen by guided tour.

Tenement Museum, 108 Orchard St; tel: 866-606-7232; www.tenement.org; tours daily, 10.30am–4pm; map C3
Eldridge Street Synagogue, 12 Eldridge St; www.eldridgestreet.org; tours Sun–Thur 10am–5pm; map B2

Catch some **hot bands in Brooklyn**, indie-music capital of the country

Because of the high concentration of bands calling the place home, Brooklyn has made its name as America's indie-music capital. The following is a list of reputable live performance spaces. (The mapping in this book doesn't extend to all of these venues, so check websites for locations.)

The Music Hall of Williamsburg (66 North 6th St, tel: 718-468-5400, www.musichallofwilliamsburg. com, map G3) features top-notch or about-to-break indie bands in a large but intimate space, run by the excellent Bowery Ballroom in Manhattan. **Pete's Candy Store** (709 Lorimer St, tel: 718-302-3770, www.petescandystore.com, off map area) is small and fun, with a hip crowd, kitsch decor, good Martinis, and live music every night. **The Brooklyn Bowl** (61 Wythe Ave, tel: 718-963-3369, www. brooklynbowl.com, map H3) is a hotspot for hearing up-and-coming bands while you try for a strike and munch on great food. **Zebulon** (258 Wythe Ave, tel: 718-218-6934, www.zebuloncafeconcert.com, map G2) has a darkly lit, laidback French cafe vibe and features great live jazz and world music ranging from reggae to Brazilian bluegrass. Some say the **Knitting Factory** (361 Metropolitan Ave, tel: 347-

529-6696, www.bk.knittingfactory. com, off map area) got its mojo back moving to Brooklyn from Manhattan. For a loud, sweaty and fun experience listening to great bands like MGMT or Bon Iver, or dancing to a DJ set, go to **Glasslands** (289 Kent Ave, www. glasslands.com, map G2).

In the more gentrified Park Slope, **Southpaw** (125 Fifth Ave, tel: 718-230-0236, www.spsounds. com, off map area) has been called 'a dive bar on steroids' and packs in crowds with its eclectic mix of live music.

Lower Manhattan and Brooklyn

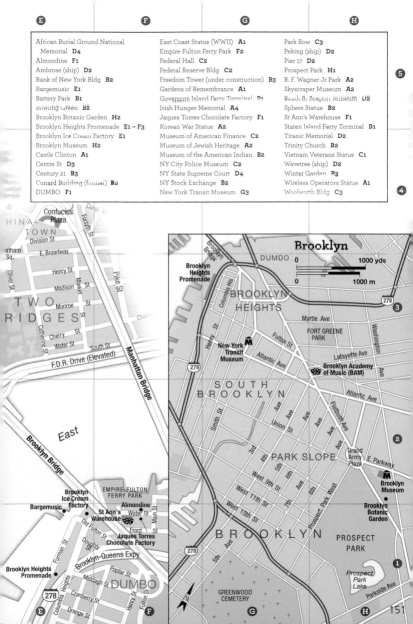

Watch the **sunset from Battery Park**, or **cruise past the Statue of Liberty** for free

A perfect place to watch the sunset over the Hudson River is from the tip of Manhattan, sitting on a stone bench on the **Battery Park Esplanade**, a pretty, green, and leafy promenade which stretches for more than a mile along the riverside. It was built with granite extracted from the same Connecticut quarry used to build the base of the Statue of Liberty in 1886 – part of a multi-million-dollar overhaul of Battery Park. Here you can also stroll through the lovely **Gardens of Remembrance**, 75,000 square feet of gardens with hundreds of varieties of plants blooming all year long, a tribute in part to victims of 9/11, designed by world-renowned Dutch horticulturalist Piet Oudolf. It's also a nod to the origins of the park: Dutch settlers in the 1600s built a low stone wall here with cannons and a battery to protect New Amsterdam from invaders.

MONUMENTS AND MEMORIALS

Battery Park pays tribute to many victims of war and suffering: a small memorial stands here for the wireless operators of the *Titanic*; victims of World War II and the Korean War are honored, as are merchant mariners lost at sea. Most poignantly, perhaps, an eternal flame burns next to *The Sphere* – Fritz Koenig's huge bronze sculpture had stood for more than 30 years in the World Trade Center Plaza, and withstood the tons of metal and concrete crashing down on top of it. In 2002, the battered globe was moved here and retitled *An Icon of Hope*, at the foot of a bed of roses called *Hope Garden*, and it is a fine spot for contemplation.

Just past the north end of the park is the **Irish Hunger Memorial**, a public artwork representing the Irish countryside with a stone cottage made from rocks from counties across Ireland – a tribute to victims of the potato famine there in the 19th century, and to all those who suffer from hunger today.

STATEN ISLAND FERRY

To get a great view of the **Statue of Liberty** from the water, avoid the long line-ups for the tourist ferries in Battery Park, and join New York commuters further south on the **Staten Island ferry**. The 25-minute cruise to Staten Island not only offers great views of the Statue of Liberty, the New York Harbor, and the city skyline, but it is also free, making it the best bargain in town (try to catch one of the old orange boats if you can as these have open decks).

Staten Island Ferry Terminal, 1 Whitehall St; www.siferry.com; departs every 20–30 mins, less frequently at off-peak times and weekends; map B1

Walk across the **Brooklyn Bridge** and tour a **chocolate factory**

There's no more dramatic way of seeing the New York skyline than crossing the **Brooklyn Bridge** on foot or by bicycle (for bike rentals *see p.98*). The world's first steel-cable suspension bridge opened in 1883 after 13 years of construction, during which 27 people lost their lives, including the principal architect John Roebling, killed by a ferryboat. Control was given to his son Washington Roebling, who fell victim to decompression sickness after surveying for the foundations of the bridge. An invalid the rest of his life, Roebling Jr monitored

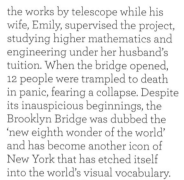

the works by telescope while his wife, Emily, supervised the project, studying higher mathematics and engineering under her husband's tuition. When the bridge opened, 12 people were trampled to death in panic, fearing a collapse. Despite its inauspicious beginnings, the Brooklyn Bridge was dubbed the 'new eighth wonder of the world' and has become another icon of New York that has etched itself into the world's visual vocabulary.

Enter the bridge in Manhattan at Centre Street and Park Row for the 20–30-minute walk over to Brooklyn. The first exit on the left deposits you in the neighborhood of DUMBO (Down Under the Manhattan Bridge Overpass). Head to the **Jacques Torres Chocolate Factory** a few blocks down Water Street, where you can watch chocolate being made through plate glass windows and indulge in handmade chocolate treats. Or, bite into a mouth-watering croissant or pastry at the **Almondine Bakery** owned by Torres across the street at no. 85.

Brooklyn Bridge; map E2
Jacques Torres Chocolate Factory, 66
Water St, Brooklyn; tel: 212-414-2462;
www.mrchocolate.com; Mon–Sat
9am–8pm, Sun 10am–6pm; map F1

Slip away to **Governors Island**

In 1614 the first Dutch settlers of New York came ashore not on Manhattan but on the small parcel of land in New York Harbor now known as Governors Island. They soon abandoned their first scrappy makeshift settlement to establish Nieuw Amsterdam at the foot of the much larger island across the East River. Since then, Governors Island has served as a fort from which cannons of the Continental Army inflicted damaged on the British fleet during the Revolutionary War, a summer retreat for colonial governors, a prison for Confederate soldiers during the Civil War, and an army and coastguard base. These days, the island is an urban getaway where visitors enjoy a 2-mile waterfront promenade, two historic fortifications (Fort Jay and Castle Williams), acres of lawns, and what may be the city's most dramatic views. The Manhattan skyline looms just a few hundred yards across the water, an endless flotilla of ships steams beneath the Verrazano Narrows Bridge, and the Statue of Liberty is dramatically near at hand, on the other side of a narrow channel – no other point of land in New York is closer to the iconic landmark.

Plans are afoot to enhance the island's low-lying landscapes with forests, marshlands, and even artificial hills and valleys. In the meantime, Governors Island is reached on a free ferry ride from the Battery Maritime Building at South and Whitehall streets in Lower Manhattan. Bikes can be rented from the **Bike and Roll** outlet on the island ($5 for 30 mins, $10 for 2 hours, and $15 for all day, free for one hour on Fridays).

Governors Island; tel: 212-825-3045; www.govisland.com; open June–early Oct Fri 10am–5pm and Sat–Sun 10am–7pm; map B1 (for ferry)

Revel in **Art Deco New York**

sense of honesty and no-nonsense efficiency, even in this more cynical age when neighboring Wall Street has displayed so much evidence to the contrary. Stepping through the vaulted, gilded, cathedral-like entrance in no way dispels these illusions: Inside is a two-story-tall banking hall, a glittering expanse of purple marble, and red-and-gold mosaics, where even cashing a check would feel like a great financial transaction.

The **Weil-Worgelt Study** is another Art Deco lair, executed by a Parisian firm of decorators for a Park Avenue apartment in 1930 and now in the **Brooklyn Museum** across the river. The olive-wood veneers, etched glass, lacquer panels, sleek furnishings, and concealed bar all suggest the very essence of urbane sophistication. You may be sorry you can't step in and lounge for a spell. The museum's wonderful collections of American art and Egyptian antiquities are just as transporting.

Even in this age of prying media, New York is still a place where it can seem that momentous and mysterious things are transpiring in the heights of mighty skyscrapers and behind closed doors. The **Bank of New York Building**, built for the Irving Bank in 1929–31, occupies one of the city's most prestigious parcels of real estate, One Wall Street. As befits the address, few buildings look more important than this Art Deco tower, its cool, clean limestone facade soaring 50 stories. The building still imparts a

Bank of New York Building; map B2
Brooklyn Museum, 200 Eastern
Parkway; tel: 718-638-5000; www.
brooklynmuseum.org; Wed–Fri 10am–
5pm, Sat–Sun 11am–6pm; Subway: 2 or 3
to Eastern Parkway; map H2

Join a former trader for an insider's look at the meltdown on **Wall Street**

Get an inside understanding of Wall Street and the financial meltdown of '08 by going on a **Financial Crisis Tour** of the area with a former investment banker who admits he traded 'toxic assets' in the days leading up to the market crash. The two-hour walking tour gives a history of the area, along with detailed explanations of Wall Street's inner workings, clocking the offices of Goldman Sachs, Deutsche Bank, and other major financial institutions as you go.

Since 9/11, the New York Stock Exchange has been closed to visitors, but the **Federal Hall National Memorial** is open to the public on weekdays. It's on the site of the original Federal Hall where, on April 30, 1789, George Washington was sworn in as the first president of the United States (there's an impressive statue of him on the steps). The original Federal Hall was demolished in 1812, and the current Greek temple-style building was put up in its place in 1836. Exhibits include a copy of the Bible used in Washington's swear-in ceremony.

The **Federal Reserve Bank**, said to hold a quarter of the world's gold reserves, also gives free tours of its vaults. Tour guides explain the history of gold and how the government stores and safeguards the billions of dollars' worth of bullion kept here.

The Wall Street Experience, tours Mon, Wed, Fri, 10am and 1.30pm, starting point, 15 Broad St; book tickets at www. wallstreetexperience.com; $50
Federal Hall National Memorial, 26 Wall St; Mon–Fri 9am–5pm; free; map C2
Federal Reserve Building, 33 Liberty St; tel: 212-720-6130; www.newyorkfed.org; tours Mon–Fri every hour 9.30am–3.30pm, except 12.30, tours must be booked in advance; free; map C2

Enjoy a concert in an extraordinary setting

Two Lower Manhattan landmarks, one old, one quite new, are stalwart survivors of the attacks of September 11. Because of their distinctive characters, they are especially appealing surroundings for performances.

Trinity Church, one of the nation's finest examples of Gothic Revival architecture, went up in 1846 beneath a steeple that long guided ships toward New York Harbor. In the aftermath of the September 11, 2001 attacks on the neighboring World Trade Center, the church filled with dust and grime, and debris fell into the adjoining, centuries-old churchyard, but Trinity was for the most part unscathed. The graceful sanctuary is especially welcoming during the classical and contemporary performances of Concerts at One, staged some weekday afternoons for the benefit of lunching Wall Streeters. The church's acclaimed choir also sings regularly, and the Trinity bell-ringers make themselves heard at the tickertape parades that traditionally march down Lower Broadway to honor heroes.

The **Winter Garden**, a glass-roofed piazza at the center of the riverside World Financial Center, was all but destroyed in the 9/11 attacks. Glass panels were shattered, and a forest of palm trees was choked in ash and cinders. The expanse of marble and glass has been rebuilt and replanted, and once again the palm-filled space stages free afternoon and evening performances, from jazz concerts to ballets to screenings of silent films accompanied by live music.

Trinity Church, 74 Trinity Place; tel: 212-602-0800; www.trinitywallstreet. org; map B2
Winter Garden, 200 Vesey St; tel: 212-417-7050; http://artsworld financialcenter.com; map B3

Experience **the avant-garde** and **Old New York** in Brooklyn

In New York-ese, DUMBO refers not to the famous flying circus elephant but to a cluster of 19th- and early 20th-century warehouses and factories tucked away Down Under the Manhattan Bridge Overpass. The iconic towers and cables of the Brooklyn Bridge, along with the Lower Manhattan skyline, are especially striking when viewed from two waterside retreats, **Empire-Fulton Ferry Park** and the **Brooklyn Bridge Park**.

DUMBO is no longer the edgy artist enclave it once was, but the avant-garde is still in evidence at **St Ann's Warehouse**, an innovative theater in a converted spice-milling factory. **Bargemusic** is an atmospheric little concert hall mounted on a former coffee barge moored at Fulton Ferry Landing. The Manhattan skyline and shimmering river are romantic backdrops for performances that run the gamut from chamber music to jazz.

Brooklyn Heights, DUMBO's neighbor, makes no pretense to being trendy. The shady streets of brick townhouse are an old-fashioned remnant of genteel New York, home to prosperous burghers who commuted by ferry to Lower Manhattan. The bench-lined **Brooklyn Heights Promenade** is the best place to enjoy the magical views across the East River, and the experience is nicely enhanced with a scoop from the **Brooklyn Ice Cream Factory** in an old fireboat station below the Promenade.

St Ann's Warehouse, 38 Water St; tel: 718-254-8779; www.stannswarehouse.org; Subway A or C to High Street; map F1
Bargemusic, Fulton Ferry Landing; tel: 718-624-2083; www.bargemusic.org; Subway A or C to High Street, 2 or 3 to Clark Street; map E1

159

Discover the wilds of **Prospect Park**, then explore the manmade world of **underground New York**

While the allure of New York is rooted in the city's manmade spectacles rather than natural beauty, **Prospect Park** has been enchanting the most diehard urbanites since the middle of the 19th century. The greensward is the city's wildest natural setting, a 585-acre parcel of forests and wetlands in the center of Brooklyn.

Prospect Park's ponds, lake, and streams are remnants of 225,000 acres of wetlands that once covered the paved-over terrain of present-day New York City and are home to all manner of plants and critters. Salamanders and toads hatch in the reedy ponds, mallards float through the grassy shallows of the lakes, hawks, herons, and hundreds of migrating birds alight in swamp azalea and willows. Long Meadow, a 60-acre pasture, winds through the center of the park and creates the illusion that you are surrounded by bucolic countryside in England or somewhere else far away from busy Brooklyn.

A far more tamed landscape prevails across Flatbush Avenue at the **Brooklyn Botanic Garden**, a contemplative and aromatic 39-acre plot of flowerbeds, rose and herb gardens, ponds, and a promenade lined with flowering cherry trees.

The **New York Transit Museum** evokes the city's greatest unnatural phenomenon, the 842-mile-long subway system. A vintage Brooklyn subway station shows off photos of the system's construction in the late 19th and early 20th centuries, the advertising that has bombarded riders over the decades, and best of all, vintage subway cars that make us realize that as much as we complain about the subway, today we ride beneath the streets in relative luxury. A shop at the museum and an annex in Grand Central Terminal are good stops for New York City souvenirs, selling such items as rain boots and umbrellas emblazoned with subway route designations.

Prospect Park; www.prospectpark.org; Subway 2 or 3 to Grand Army Plaza; map H1
Brooklyn Botanic Garden, 900 Washington Ave; tel: 718-623-7200; www.bbg.org; mid-Mar–Nov,

*Tue–Fri 8am–6pm, Sat–Sun 10am–6pm;
children under-12 free; Subway: B or
Q to Prospect Park, 2 or 3 to Eastern
Parkway, or B, F, Q, and S to Prospect
Park Station; map H2
New York Transit Museum, Corner
of Boerum Place/Schemmerhorn St,
Brooklyn Heights; tel: 718-694-1600;
Tue–Fri 10am–4pm, Sat–Sun noon–5pm;
Subway: Borough Hall; map G3*

A TREE GROWS IN THE BRONX
One of the world's finest botanical
gardens flourishes on 250 acres in
the Bronx. The **New York Botanical
Garden** harbors 1 million plants
in 50 cultivated gardens and a
50-acre native forest that evokes
New York as it appeared to Native
American inhabitants and early
settlers. A tropical climate prevails
in the Enid A. Haupt Conservatory,
an enormous Victorian greenhouse
where rainforest plants, cacti, and
palm trees thrive beneath acres of
glass panels. By train, you can reach
the gardens from Grand Central
Terminal, getting off at the Botanical
Garden Station. By subway, take
the B, D, or 4 trains to the Bedford
Park Blvd Station and walk (about
15 minutes) or take the Bx26 bus.
(Bronx River Parkway at Forham Rd,
tel: 718-817-8700, www.nybg.org;
Tue–Sun 10am–6pm).

Pay homage to the **skyscraper** and to those who lost their lives as **slaves in colonial New York**

In this, the most vertical of cities, **The Skyscraper Museum** pays homage to the pivotal role of the high-rise in the development of the city. Through exhibitions, programs, and publications, the small museum explores tall buildings as objects of design, products of technology, sites of construction, and places of work and residence. The dazzling interior (*pictured p.148*) uses polished stainless-steel floors and ceilings to give a sense of towering canyons. Temporary exhibits feature architectural models and photographs showcasing the evolution of skyscrapers; permanent exhibits pay tribute to the World Trade Center and the current rebuilding plans.

The **African Burial Ground National Memorial** commemorates those who laid down the first foundations of the city. In 1991, when workers were excavating the foundations of a new Federal courthouse building, the skeletons of about 400 men, women, and children were found. The site, it transpired, was part of a colonial burial ground for slaves. The memorial was erected in 2007 to honor an estimated 15,000 slaves buried here from the beginnings of New York as a Dutch colony in the 1600s to the abolition of slavery in 1865.

The Skyscraper Museum, 39 Battery Place; tel: 212 968-1961; www.skyscraper. org; Wed–Sun, 12pm–6pm; charge; map A2

The African Burial Ground National Memorial, corner of Duane St/Elk St; daily 9am–5pm; free; map D4

Be awed by the **Woolworth Building**, a neo-Gothic Cathedral of Commerce

From 1913 to 1930, the 792-foot-tall **Woolworth Building** was the tallest manmade structure in the world. Though many other skyscrapers have long since soared higher, few can match the white neo-Gothic tower for grace and style. The great retailer, Frank W. Woolworth, paid cash for the construction, a cool $13.5 million, and by that time the former farm boy had so much clout that President Woodrow Wilson joined the opening ceremonies, switching on the building's 80,000 lights from his desk in the White House.

Woolworth created an empire of close to 600 stores, where every item sold for five or ten cents – the 'five-and-dimes' that have since disappeared from the American landscape. Woolworth's respect for the value of a dollar is captured in one the lobby paintings, where he is depicted counting nickels. Not that Woolworth was a penny-pincher, as the ornate mosaic tiles, acres of marble, and gold-leafed cornices in his so-called Cathedral of Commerce attest. He was downright extravagant when it came to his own comforts, building an estate on Long Island that required the services of an army of servants. His most famous descendant was granddaughter Barbara Hutton. Once the world's richest woman, her seven husbands included princes, barons, and the actor Cary Grant.

You can only peer into the ornate Woolworth lobby from the entrance, but you may muse on commerce and fortunes as you gaze upon the tower from the monumental steps of the **New York State Supreme Court** (60 Centre St, map D4). If the surroundings seem familiar, that's because they appear in the opening of the long-running television show *Law and Order*.

Woolworth Building, 233 Broadway; map C3

Set sail across **New York Harbor**

Time was, some 200 years ago, that the South Street Seaport bustled with seafaring commerce. It's possible to recapture some of that old-time ambience on the quaintly cobbled, shop-lined lanes. A fleet of the vessels that once filled New York Harbor with their acres of canvas sails and smokestacks are berthed at docks that are part of the **South Street Seaport Museum**. Dockside galleries are filled with photographs and other mementoes of seafaring days of yore. Among the ships that can be boarded are the *Peking*, a clipper from 1911 and one of the largest sailing ships ever built; the *Wavetree*, a fully rigged wrought-iron vessel that saw duty carrying jute for rope-making from Bangladesh to Scotland; and the *Ambrose*, a lightship that once guided mariners across the sandbars in the mouth of New York Bay.

Harbor cruises set off from the seaport aboard the *Pioneer*, a late 19th-centry cargo sloop, and the *Lettie G. Howard*, a fishing schooner. The *W. O. Decker*, a 1930s tugboat, pokes through the backwaters of New York Harbor. Two historic craft of Manhattan by Sail, the *Sheerwater* and *Clipper City*, also ply the harbor, with daytime, twilight, and evening cruises (tel: 212-619-0907, 800-544-1224, www.manhattanbysail.com).

South Street Seaport Museum, 12 Fulton St; tel: 212-748-8600, www.southstreetmuseumseaport.org; Jan–Mar Fri–Mon 10am–5pm, ships noon–4pm, April–Dec Tues–Sun 10am–6pm; map D2

Discover works of **American Indian art**, and shop for fine **handcrafted jewelry**

The little-known, and blissfully uncrowded **Museum of the American Indian** operated by the Smithsonian Institution, showcases highlights from the vast collection of Native art and artifacts assembled by investment banker and oil heir George Gustav Heye in the late 19th and early 20th centuries. The small selection of Indian headdresses, moccasins, bows, arrows, masks, and Indian art offers a particularly intimate glimpse into a rich cultural and artistic tradition. Many staff members are Native Americans, from tribal groups across the hemisphere, and their firsthand knowledge (and willingness to impart it) is a far cry from the typical museum experience.

Also atypical is the museum's setting in the city's finest example of Beaux-Arts architecture designed by Cass Gilbert, also responsible for the city's first skyscraper, the nearby Woolworth Building *(see p. 163)*. The four impressive sculptures that flank the facade, representing Asia, America, Europe, and Africa, were the work of David Chester French, the artist who created the even larger statue of Abraham Lincoln for Washington's Lincoln Memorial. Below the cornices at the top of the building are 12 statues honoring seafaring nations and cities around the world. Inside are soaring ceilings, a beautiful rotunda and marble work, and murals that depict the early explorers of America.

Rounding off your visit nicely, the exceptional museum shop sells beautiful handcrafted jewelry and woolen blankets, and an array of good books and cards.

Museum of the American Indian; 1 Bowling Green; tel: 212-514-3700; www.nmai.si.edu; daily 10am–5pm, Thur until 8pm; free; map B2

Take a reflective walk around the **World Trade Center** site

Roughly a decade after the collapse of the World Trade Center, the site remains a political battle zone, with construction progress slowed by arguments and power struggles between city and state officials, developers, and groups wanting respect for the victims of the 9/11 attack. The ambitious overall plan is for five new office towers to go up, including the Freedom Tower that will reach the symbolic height of 1,776 feet – the number being the year the US Declaration of Rights was signed. There will also be an arts centre,

a memorial museum, and visitor's centre. The best view of the cranes at work is from the windows of the World Financial Center across the street: from a public hallway you can see the footprints of the original towers that will be surrounded by fields of trees and filled with pools of water. Names of the victims will be written along the edges of the pools in this tribute called 'Reflecting Absence.'

To learn more about the site and about 9/11, you can take a 75-minute tour led by people whose lives were involved in the tragedy, such as rescue workers, survivors, and residents of Lower Manhattan. The $10 tours depart from 120 Liberty Street four times a day.

To see moving photos taken by firemen and poignant artifacts from the collapse, take a 10-minute taxi ride to the **Ground Zero Museum Workshop** in the Meatpacking District. Part of the $25 ticket proceeds go to charities associated with 9/11 and the fire department.

World Trade Center site; tours: www. tributewtc.org; map B3
Ground Zero Museum Workshop, 420 W. 14th St; www.groundzeromuseum. com; advance online purchase of tickets required; map p.78 B3

Find a bargain at a **discount designer emporium**

The sign outside the **Century 21** building that sits on the eastern edge of the World Trade Center site says 'New York's Best Kept Secret,' but once you enter this madhouse of shoppers looking for bargains, you'll wonder who is it exactly that doesn't know about this place? There's a reason it's crowded: several floors of designer men's, ladies' and children's wear at slashed prices. Come armed with patience and a clear head to sort through racks and racks of pants, tops, dresses, suits, ties, and shirts, and pay attention to the price tags: even though the discounts here can be two-thirds off the original price, they are still high when the list price for a dress is $1,100.

Coming very early on a weekday is your best way to avoid a shopping meltdown if you're prone to them.

Loehmann's (101 Seventh Ave between 16th/17th sts, Mon–Sat, 9am–9pm, Sun 11am–7pm; map p.78 C3) in Chelsea can be a less harried place to shop for discounted clothes, shoes, and handbags, but also requires patience and focus. Like Century 21, it features slashed prices on designer names, but there are more mass-market, therefore cheaper items. Avoid weekend afternoons.

Century 21, 22 Cortlandt St; www. c21stores.com; Mon–Wed 7.45am–8pm, Thur–Fri 7.45am–10pm, Sat 10am–8pm; Sun 11am–7pm; map B3

hotels

As gentrification transforms one Manhattan neighborhood after another, the hotel scene continues to push into new territory. Even the once grimy Lower East Side and Meatpacking District now have some places to lay your head in chic comfort.

Where you choose to stay, though, still comes down to good old-fashioned common sense. In this city where walking is the easiest way to get from point A to point B, you'll want to lodge where the center of your particular kind of action is. If you plan on making the rounds of clubs till dawn, you'll probably want to be downtown. If your idea of a good time is a day in a museum and a night at the opera, the Upper East Side and Upper West Side are the places to be. Midtown, as always, is ideal for shopping and theatergoing.

As the roster of hotels grows longer, so do the list of amenities. Spas, in-house gyms or temporary passes to health clubs, flat screens, Wi-Fis, iPod docks, and other privileges and gizmos are fairly standard equipment these days. Some also offer an amenity that's especially welcome in one of the most expensive cities in the world – good value at a fair price.

HOTEL PRICES
A standard room in peak season

$$$$ over $400
$$$ $250–400
$$ $150–250
$ under $150

Hip Havens

The Ace Hotel
Chelsea/Flatiron
20 W. 29th St; tel: 212-679-2222; www. acehotel/newyork.com; map p79 E4; $$–$$$

Combine the old-world charm of 1904 surroundings with a boho-chic vibe and what do you get? Hipster heaven that brings together taxidermy, old tiles, over-sized couches, library desks, and great coffee. Throw in a fashionable bar (The Breslin), a laptop filled lobby and a nightclub lounge downstairs, and the Ace trumps.

The Cooper Square Hotel
Greenwich Village/East Village
25 Cooper Square; tel: 212-475-5700; www. thecoopersquarehotel.com; map p97 F2; $$$$

Both humans and dogs are well-catered to here: free champagne on arrival for Homo sapiens, room service for their canine companions. Floor-to-ceiling windows ensure views from the 20 floors, and a hip bar and restaurant and rooftop patio ensure plenty of socializing for the two-legged set.

Hotel on Rivington
East Village/Lower East Side
107 Rivington St.; tel: 212-475-2600; www. hotelonrivington.com; map p132 C3; $$$$

It only stands to reason that glamorous lodgings would arrive on the Lower East Side – one of the last holdouts of gritty New York is now trendy, and guests who wish to enjoy the nearby clubs and restaurants can surround themselves with chic style and, from the upper floors, movie-worthy views of the city.

The Standard New York Hotel
Meatpacking District

848 Washington St; tel: 212-645-4646;
www.standardhotels.com/new-york-city;
map p96 B5; $$$$

Straddling the High Line (*p.88*), the
too-chic-for-words Standard pulls in the
international fashion crowd like honey
draws bees. The restaurant and three
bars are casually glamorous, but the
sensational views of the city and the
Hudson River from the high-ceilinged
rooms are uniquely New York.

Hudson Hotel
Midtown

356 W. 58th St; tel: 212-554-6000; www.
hudsonhotel.com; map p58 D5; $$–$$$

The guestrooms are minuscule, but the
premises are so urbanely sophisticated
that size doesn't matter to most style-
fixated guests, who prefer to spend
their time in the stunning public areas
– a book-lined library with fireplace and
pool table, a bar with glowing floor and
ceiling mural by Francesco Clemente,
and a sumptuous terrace garden

The Maritime Hotel
Meatpacking District/Chelsea

363 W. 16th St; tel: 212-242-4300; www.
themaritimehotel.com; map p78 B3; $$–$$$

A former retirement home for sailors,
complete with porthole-shaped
windows, is these days a favorite with
the entertainment biz. The rooms and
lobby play to the nautical theme with
teak furnishings, white walls, and cabin-
size rooms. Some of the public spaces
are so dark you'll feel you're below
decks, but a cocktail on the patio can
be as refreshing as a sea breeze.

Heart of the Action

The Paramount Hotel
■ Midtown
235 W. 46th St; tel: 212-764-5500; www.
nycparamount.com; map p58 D3; $$
The Zeitgeist seems to have departed
from what was once a pioneer of the
cutting-edge lodging scene. What
remains are clean, affordable, no-frills
rooms in the middle of the theater
district.

Royalton
■ Midtown
44 W. 44th St; tel: 212-869-4400; www.
royaltonhotel.com; map p59 E2; $$
Philippe Starck's first foray into
hospitality design was the trailblazer
for a wave of high-style hotels to
follow. A recent renovation has
altered the original aesthetics
somewhat, but the Royalton still sets
the gold standard for quality, stylish
accommodation and excellent service.

The W Union Square
■ Flatiron
201 Park Ave S; tel: 212-253-9119; www.
whotelsnewyork.com; map p79 E2; $$$
The chain that introduced the concept
of contemporary chic to the New York
hotel scene still sets a high standard
with stunningly designed rooms, many
creature comforts, and a hip, clubby
atmosphere. This one is close to the
Village, Lower East Side, and other
downtown enclaves, but within easy
reach of Midtown, too (where two other
equally stylish Ws are located).

Urban Hideaways

Inn at Irving Place
🔲 **Gramercy Park**

56 Irving Place; tel: 212-533-4600; www.
innatirving.com; map p79 E2; $$$$

Irving Place is one of the last bastions
of Old New York, and stepping through
the doors of this 12-room inn involves
a bit of time travel. Those in search
of cutting-edge style will do well to
look elsewhere, but the antiques-filled
milieu, afternoon tea, and personalized
service will suit any traveler looking to
indulge in gentler times.

Library Hotel
🔲 **Midtown**

299 Madison Ave; tel: 212-983-4500; www.
libraryhotel.com; map p59 E1; $$–$$$

The nearby New York Public Library
inspires this unique Midtown oasis,
where lounges and guestrooms are
filled with books. You can choose your
room according to a subject of interest
to you (literature, science, erotica).
Guests enjoy complimentary coffee,
tea, and evening cheese and wine in the
welcoming lounges and terraces.

The Franklin
🔲 **Upper East Side**

164 E. 87th St; tel: 212-369-1000, 800-607-
4009; map p25 G4; $$

Flowerboxes on the facade of a
nondescript building on a bland side
street only hint at the warmth and
style that lies within. Small rooms
are enhanced with tasteful decor,
comfortable beds, and a slew of other
amenities. The area is chockablock
with shops and restaurants, and Fifth
Avenue museums and Central Park are
just a short stroll away.

The Mercer
🔲 **Soho**

147 Mercer St; tel: 212-966-6060; www.
mercerhotel.com; map p117 E4; $$$$

If you want to feel like a star, you can
do no better than this Soho retreat
that's the final word in contemporary
chic and discretion. Lavish rooms
and suites are filled with handsome
designer furnishings, sumptuous
bathrooms, and every electronic
gismo imaginable. The in-house
restaurant, Mercer Kitchen, does the
premises justice.

Landmarks

Algonquin Hotel
■ Midtown

59 W. 44th St; tel: 212-840-6800; www.
algonquinhotel.com; map p. 58 E2; $$–$$$

Steeped in literary tradition, this
century-plus-old landmark surrounds
guests with plenty of solid, old-
fashioned comfort. The premises evoke
the days when *New Yorker* magazine
staffers and other literati tossed
witticisms around the homey lobby bar
– still a welcoming place to sink into an
armchair, a resident cat on your lap.

The Carlyle
■ Upper East Side

35 E. 76th St; tel: 212-744-1600; www.
thecarlyle.com; map p25 F3; $$$$

The great bastion of Old New York
caters to royals, politicians, and
other elites, housing them in refined
Art Deco-inspired guestrooms and
pampering them with attentive service.
Bemelman's Bar *(p. 35)* allows non-
guests to get a whiff of the elegance
that prevails, and the Café Carlyle is a
highly acclaimed music venue.

Hotel Chelsea
■ Chelsea

222 W. 23rd St; tel. 212-243-3700; www.
hotelchelsea.com; map p.78 C4; $$

Legendary crash pad of musicians like
Leonard Cohen and Janis Joplin, and
Arthur Miller who penned plays here,
and where artists still come to paint,
write, or make films. Don't expect usual
hotel services (you'll be lucky to get a
hairdryer in your room), but do expect
an authentic bohemian environment, a
rarity in gentrified Manhattan.

St Regis

Midtown
2 E. 55th St; tel: 212-753-4500; www.
stregisnewyork.com; map p.59 F4; $$$$

One of the world's legendary hostelries,
built by Colonel John Jacob Astor just
before he went down on the *Titanic*.
Acres of marble, crystal, and silk
provide some of the city's swankiest
surroundings. Fifth Avenue shopping is
just outside the door and the King Cole
Bar is a tempting place to idle away the
hours (*p.69*).

Waldorf-Astoria Hotel

Midtown
301 Park Ave; tel: 212-355-3000; www.
waldorfastoria.com; map p.59 F3; $$$–$$$$

You almost expect to hear someone
playing Gershwin on the piano when
you walk into the lobby, a bustling Art
Moderne extravaganza that captures
the essence of mid-20th-century New
York. The years have taken away some
of that Walforf charm, but plenty of
flourish prevails, and the Park Avenue
address is very grand indeed.

Hotel Pennsylvania

Midtown
401 Seventh Ave; tel: 212-736-5000; www.
hotelpenn.com; map p.58 C1; $$

Glenn Miller immortalized the phone
number (back in the days of named
prefixes, it was Pennsylvania 6-5000)
in the 1940s, when this vast complex
of ballrooms and guestrooms was the
largest hotel in the world. The place is
still huge, and though rooms are a bit
bland and anonymous, they are good
value and close to Midtown attractions.

Lap of Luxury

Gramercy Park Hotel
■ Gramercy

2 Lexington Ave; tel. 212-920-3300; www.
gramercyparkhotel.com; map p.79 F3; $$$$

Stylish opulence prevails from the
moment you step into the elegant
lobby and lounge designed by film
director and artist Julian Schnabel.
The well-heeled clientele from around
the world get a key to Gramercy Park
to take a stroll where few New Yorkers
get to go (p.84).

Mandarin Oriental
■ Midtown

Time Warner Center; 80 Columbus Circle;
tel: 212-805-8800; www.mandarinoriental.
com; map p.58 E5; $$$$

Stunning views of Central Park and the
Midtown skyline fill the floor-to-ceiling
windows in all the quietly glamorous,
Asian-influenced rooms. The spa is
fabulous, and the many other in-house
amenities are topped off with the
restaurants, bars, and shops of the
Time Warner Center below.

Soho Grand
■ Soho

310 West Broadway; tel: 212-965-3000;
www.sohogrand.com; map p.116 D3; $$$$

One of the first luxury downtown
hotels (opened in 1996) still holds
its own as a trendsetter and crowd-
pleaser. For those looking for more than
contemporary, stylish surroundings
and hip bars and lounges, the Grand
adds a few quirky twists to its long list
of amenities – pets are welcome, and
goldfish are provided to those who
don't have one.

Classic Comfort

Excelsior Hotel
Upper West Side

45 W. 81st St; tel: 212-362-9200; map p.24 D4; $$–$$$

Most New Yorkers can only dream about living in one of the grand old apartment houses facing the Natural History Museum, and here's your chance to call the block home. Leather, marble and paneling provide old-world elegance, but the real perks are space (all rooms are suites) and glimpses of Central Park just down the street.

Hotel Wales
Upper East Side

1295 Madison Ave; tel: 866-925-3746; www.waleshotel.com; map p.25 G5; $$–$$$

Solid, old-fashioned comfort pervades this perennial favorite of legions of return guests who love the proximity to the Upper East Side museums. The elegant stretch of Upper Madison is a bit removed from other city attractions, but the rooftop terrace, in-house dining at popular Sarabeth's, and a comfy library/lounge make a perfect getaway.

Lucerne Hotel
Upper West Side

201 West 79th St; tel: 212-875-1000; www.thelucernehotel.com; map p.24 C4; $$–$$$

This century-old landmark is popular not only for its homey, traditionally furnished rooms and excellent service, but for the Lincoln Center, the American Museum of Natural History, and the many other attractions that lie just outside the door. The in-house restaurant, Nice Matin, is one of the neighborhood's favorite spots for a drink or meal.

No Frills, Good Value

Inn on 23rd Street
■ Chelsea

131 W. 23rd St; tel: 212-463-0330, 877-387-2323; www.innon23rd.com; map p.78 D4; $$

Imagine coming to Manhattan and staying in a friend's tasteful, idiosyncratically decorated townhouse. That's the feel of this converted home in the heart of hip Chelsea. The various motifs – rustic Americana, Victorian, 1940s – along with a sumptuous breakfast, make this a place you would happily return to on your next visit.

Blue Moon Hotel
■ Lower East Side

100 Orchard St; tel: 212-533-9080; www.bluemoon-nyc.com; map p.132 C2; $$

A renovated tenement evokes the warmth and color of the Lower East Side with architectural artifacts, collages, and a stylishly bohemian flair. These commodious, laidback rooms capture the spirit of what is quickly being revitalized as one of the city's trendiest neighborhoods.

Marrakech
■ Upper West Side

2688 Broadway; tel: 212-222-2954; www.marrakechhotelnyc.com; off map; $–$$

A Moroccan theme prevails in the lobby/cocktail lounge and the deep hues of the small but comfortable rooms. The restaurants and attractions of the Upper West Side are nearby, but the greatest appeal is value – quality at this price is a rare commodity in Manhattan. Note there is no elevator, but valets are on hand to help with bags.

Pod Hotel
Midtown
230 E. 50th St; tel: 866-414-4617; www.
podhotel.com; map p.59 G2; $–$$
Welcome aboard. Bunk beds, lots of
shiny chrome, shared baths, space-is-at-
a-premium touches, and tiny individual
flat screens lend the sense that you're
on an airliner – or, better yet, a space-
ship. Quarters are tight, but the price
is right, and you'll get a sense of how
most space-starved Manhattanites live.

Washington Square Hotel
Greenwich Village
103 Waverly Place; tel: 212-777-9515; www.
washingtonsquarehotel.com; map p.97 D3;
$–$$
Decades have passed since writers and
artists found their haven in what was, in
the words of the Joan Baez song, 'that
crummy hotel overlooking Washington
Square.' Rooms are still on the small
side, and most overlook a brick wall,
but the accommodation is comfortable,
affordable, and in a great location.

The Larchmont
Greenwich Village
27 W. 11th St; tel: 212-989-9333; www.
larchmonthotel.com; map p.97 E4; $
It's hard to beat the lovely peaceful
stretch of a tree- and brownstone-
lined street for location, but leave any
notion of elegance at the doorstep. The
surroundings are simple in decor and
spare in services and facilities (toilets
and showers are shared), but the place
is attractive and clean, and one of the
best hotel deals in this expensive city.

Essentials

A

Airports and Arrival

New York's two major airports, **John F. Kennedy** and **LaGuardia**, are respectively 15 and 8 miles (24 and 13km) from Manhattan. Driving time to the airports is just under one hour, but heavy traffic can easily double this. The metropolitan area's third major airport, **Newark Liberty** International, is actually in New Jersey, but for many New Yorkers it can be more convenient than either JFK or LaGuardia.

The **New York Airport Service** (tel: 212-875-8200) operates buses to and from Manhattan, JFK, and LaGuardia. Pick up and drop-off points include: the Port Authority Bus Terminal, Penn Station, and Grand Central Terminal.

New Jersey Transit (tel: 973-275-5555) and Coach USA (tel: 877-8-NEWARK) operate express buses between Newark Airport and the Port Authority Bus Terminal, Penn Station, Grand Central Terminal, and Lower Manhattan. A minibus service from all three airports to many Manhattan hotels is provided by **Super Shuttle Blue Vans** (tel: 800-258-3826), offering door-to-door transportation.

AirTrain is a rail system connecting JFK and Newark airports with the subway and railway network. AirTrain JFK information: tel: 877-535-2478; www.airtrainjfk.com. AirTrai n Newark: tel: 888-397 4636; www.panynj.gov/airports/ewr-airtrain.html.

C

Climate

New York City has four distinct seasons and is at its best in spring and fall. Summer temperatures hover in the upper 70s° to upper 80s°F (24°–29°C), but temperatures in excess of 90°F (32°C) are not uncommon. Expect uncomfortable humidity in July and August. September and October sometimes usher in a balmy, dry 'Indian summer' that fills parks and office plazas with sun worshippers. Winter temperatures often drop below freezing and, with the wind chill factor, can feel much colder. The average temperature in January is 32°F (0°C). Heavy snowfall occasionally snarls traffic, although snow-removal crews are relatively efficient. Average annual rainfall is 44in (112cm); average snowfall is 29 in (74cm). Raincoats and umbrellas are a good idea year-round.

D

Disabled Access

Disabled travelers can obtain information about rights and special facilities from the Mayor's Office for People with Disabilities (tel: 212-788-2830; www.nyc.gov/mopd).

E

Electricity

Standard American electric current is

110 volts. An adapter is necessary for European appliances, which run on 220–240 volts.

Embassies and consulates
Australia Mission to the UN, 150 East 42nd Street, tel: 212-351-6600.
British Consulate-General, 845 Third Avenue, tel: 212-745-0200.
Canadian Consulate-General, 1251 Sixth Avenue, tel: 212-596-1783.
Consulate General of Ireland, 345 Park Avenue, tel: 212-319-2555.
New Zealand Consulate, 222 East 41st Street, tel: 212-832-4038
Consulate of South Africa, 333 East 38th Street, tel: 212-213-4880.

Emergencies
Police, fire, ambulance, tel: 911.
Dental emergency, tel: 212-486-9458.
Sex Crimes Report Line, tel: 212-267-7273.

Entry regulations
Due to increased security, the precise regulations for entry to the United States change often, and vary for citizens of different countries. It's a good idea to check on the current situation before you travel, on http://travel.state.gov or via a US Embassy or Consulate in your home country. And remember the US has strict rules on liquids in carry-on luggage, so check with your airline before you fly.

G
Gay and Lesbian
Historically, the epicenter of New York's gay community has been Greenwich Village; the West Village in particular, but in recent years, however, the community's center of gravity has shifted north to neighboring Chelsea. Eight Avenue in particular, between 14th and 23rd streets, is lined with bars catering to a gay clientele.

Useful Resources
Gay and Lesbian Hotline, tel: 212-989-0999; Mon–Fri 4pm–12pm, Sat noon–5pm. Provides information about all aspects of gay life in New York, including recommendations for bars, restaurants, legal counseling, etc.
Lesbian, Gay, Bisexual and Transgender Community Center, 208 West 13th Street (at Seventh Avenue); tel: 212-620-7310; www.gaycenter.org; daily 9am–11pm. This large and helpful organization offers a wide range of services and events, ranging from educational conferences, and political action to dances and parties.
Gay City News, gaycitynews.com. A newspaper covering local, national, and international news and events.

H
Health and Medical Care
Medical services are extremely expensive. Purchase comprehensive

travel insurance to cover any emergencies. **Physicians Home Care**, tel: 718-238 2100 www.doctorinthefamily.com, for non-emergency house calls. To find a local pharmacy, go to www.cvs.com or www.duanereade.com. Both drugstores have many locations throughout the city, with varying hours.

Hospitals with emergency rooms
Bellevue Hospital, First Avenue and East 27th Street; tel: 212-562-4141.
Beth Israel Medical Center, First Avenue at 16th St; tel: 212-420-2840.
NYU Medical Center, 550 First Avenue at 33rd Street; tel: 212-263-7300.
St Luke's-Roosevelt Hospital, 59th Street at Tenth avenue; tel: 212-523-6800.
Columbia Presbyterian Medical Center, 630 West 168th Street; tel: 212-305-2500.
Lenox Hill Hospital, 100, East 77th Street at Park Avenue; tel: 212-434-2000.
Mount Sinai Hospital, Fifth Avenue and 100th Street; tel: 212-241-6500.
New York Hospital, 525 East 68th Street; tel: 212-746-5454.

I
Internet
Free wi-fi internet access is available in thousands of hotspots across the city including hotels, cafes, city parks and train stations. For the latest update check out www.wififreespot.com. Email can be sent from most branches of FedEx-Kinko's copy shops or from branches of the New York Public Library, including the Science, Industry, and Business Library, 188 Madison Ave at 34th St, tel: 212-592 7000.

L
Lost Property
The chances of retrieving lost property are not high, but the occasional civic-minded individual may turn items in to the nearest police precinct.
To inquire about items left on public transportation (subway and bus), tel: 212-712-4500, open Mon, Tue, Fri 8am–noon, Wed, Thur 11am–6.45pm. Or call 311.
Lost or stolen credit cards
American Express, tel: 1-800-528 4800.
Diners Club, tel: 1-800-234 6377.
MasterCard, tel: 1-800-826 2181.
Visa, tel: 1-800-847 2911.
All 1-800 calls are free of charge.

M
Maps
NYC & Co has good maps at their visitor center (810 Seventh Avenue between 52nd and 53rd streets) and online at www.nycgo.com.. Subway and bus maps are available at subway station booths, or from the New York City Transit Authority booth in

Grand Central Terminal and the Long Island Rail Road information booth in Penn Station, as well as the MTA booth at the Times Square Visitors Center. You can also download them from www.mta.info. The most detailed street map is a book called *Manhattan Block by Block*, published by Tauranac Maps.

Street Grid

Generally, in midtown and uptown Manhattan, avenues run north to south; streets run east to west. Even-numbered streets tend to have one-way eastbound traffic; odd-numbered streets, westbound traffic. There are notable exceptions such as 14th and 23rd streets, which have two-way traffic. Most avenues are one-way, either north or south, the major exception being Park Avenue which has two-way traffic north of 44th Street.

The picture is more confusing in Greenwich Village and other downtown neighborhoods, where most of the streets have names instead of numbers and run at all angles.

Media

Print

The *New York Times* and *Wall Street Journal* are both regarded as papers of national significance, and they are also strong on local issues. The Times' bulky Sunday edition has extensive coverage of local arts and entertainment.

Two papers compete for the tabloid market: the *New York Post* and the *Daily News*. There are two 'commuter' dailies distributed free in the mornings: *AM New York* and *Metro*. The free alternative weekly *Village Voice* has comprehensive listings and classified ads, as does the *New York Observer* and *New York Press*. Local magazines with extensive event listings include *New York* and *Time Out New York* (see also websites for good sources of local news and listings information).

Radio

There are more than 70 radio stations in New York City. Some of the better stations with local news include:

WNYC	93.9FM/820AM
WABC	770AM
WCBS	880AM
WINS	1010AM
WBBR	1130AM

Television

The three major networks – all with New York headquarters – are ABC (77 West 66th Street; tel: 212-456-7777), CBS (51 West 52nd Street; tel: 212-975-4321), and NBC (30 Rockefeller Plaza; tel: 212-664-4444). Fox News has a national office at 1211 Sixth Avenue (tel: 212-556-2500), and CNN has offices at the Time Warner Center at Columbus Circle. The Public Broadcasting Service (PBS) can be found on channels 13 and 21 on the

VHF band (for those without cable). The other three local stations are affiliated with the Fox (5), UPN (9), and WB (11) networks. These channels broadcast nationally aired shows as well as local programming. In addition, half a dozen UHF stations broadcast in Spanish and other languages.

Various cable companies offer 50 or more basic cable and movie channels, although the number varies depending on the service provider.

Money

Most ATMs will charge a fee for withdrawing cash. Credit cards are accepted almost everywhere in the city, although not all cards are accepted at all places.

There are numerous outlets for exchanging currency and cashing traveler's checks in New York. Travelex, tel: 800-287-7362; 1590 Broadway at 48th Street, tel: 212-265-6063; 1271 Broadway at 32nd Street, tel: 212-679-4877; and 511 Madison Avenue at 53rd Street, tel: 212-753-0117.

There are numerous American Express offices around town, including 374 Park Avenue, tel: 212-421 8240; 111 Broadway, tel: 212-693-1100; 3 World Financial Center, tel: 212-640-5130; and 151 West 34th Street, tel: 212-695-8075. There is also an automated self-change kiosk at the Times Square Information Center at 1560 Broadway (between 46th and 47th streets).

Citibank offers exchange facilities at most of its 200 or so branches around the five boroughs. Tel: 800-285-3000.

Refunds
Department stores usually allow you to return merchandise up to 30 days after purchase for full credit. Boutiques are less accommodating; some allow store credit only, and no returns or exchanges after seven days.

Museums and Galleries

Visitors will find that pretty much everywhere and every attraction in New York charges an entrance fee. Some of these are surprisingly expensive, especially the major galleries: MoMA and the Met are $20 each; the Guggenheim and the Whitney cost $18; and the Museum of Natural History is $16.

As with restaurants, stores, and clubs, galleries spring up overnight and disappear just as quickly. Consult the listings magazines, as well as the art section of the *New York Times* on Friday and Sunday. A free monthly *Gallery Guide* can be picked up at various arty locations. Or look up what's on where at www.artinfo.com/galleryguide. Note that most galleries are closed on Mondays.

P

Postal Services

Manhattan's main post office is on

Eighth Avenue between 31st and 33rd streets; it is open 24 hours a day. To locate post offices elsewhere in the five boroughs, call 800-275-8777 or go to www.usps.com.

Public Holidays

The US has shifted most public holidays to the Monday closest to the actual dates, thereby creating a number of three-day weekends. Holidays that are observed no matter the day on which they fall are:
New Year's Day (January 1).
Independence Day (July 4).
Veterans' Day (November 11).
Christmas Day (December 25).

Other holidays are:
Martin Luther King Jr Day (third Mon in Jan).
President's Day (third Mon in Feb).
Memorial Day (last Mon in May).
Labor Day (first Mon in Sep).
Columbus Day (second Mon in Oct).
Election Day (first Tues in Nov, every four years).
Thanksgiving (fourth Thur in Nov).

T

Taxis

Taxis, all metered, cruise the streets and must be hailed, although there are designated taxi stands at places like Grand Central Terminal and Penn Station. Be sure to flag down an official yellow cab, not an unlicensed gypsy cab. The flat rate for a taxi between JFK and Manhattan is $45 plus tolls.

One fare covers up to four passengers (five in some larger cabs). There is a small surcharge on all taxi rides from 4pm to 8pm on weekdays.

New York Water Taxis provide ferry service on the Hudson and East rivers. In addition to daily commuter service between Manhattan, Brooklyn and Queens, water taxis offer scenic tours, birdwatching tours and sunset cruises with live music. See www.nywatertaxi.com for information.

Telephones

Most Manhattan locations have a 212 area code. Brooklyn, Queens, Staten Island, and Bronx numbers are prefixed by 718 (or the newer 347 or 917). Regardless of the number you are calling from, the area code of the number being called must now be used and preceded by 1.
Toll-free calls are prefixed by 800, 888 or 877; remember to dial 1 first when calling these numbers.

Telephones accepting credit cards can be found in various centers, including Grand Central Terminal and Penn Station. Hotels also usually add a hefty surcharge. Telephone dialing cards, available widely in convenience stores and elsewhere, are an inexpensive way to make calls.

essentials

Useful Numbers

Useful Numbers
International calls, dial 011 (the international access code), then the country code, city code, and local number.
Directory help, dial 555-1212 preceded by the area code you are calling from, or 411.
Emergencies, dial 911.

Non-Emergency Services
New York has a three-digit number to be dialed for information and non-emergency services. Calls to 311 are answered by a live operator 24 hours a day, seven days a week, and services are provided in over 170 languages. Operators are prepared to respond to a wide range of calls, including tourist inquiries, complaints about noise, queries about public transportation, and information about lost items.

Time zone

New York observes Eastern Standard Time (EST). This is five hours behind London, one hour ahead of Chicago, and three hours ahead of California.

Tipping

Most New Yorkers in the service industries regard tips as a God-given right, not just a pleasant gratuity. The fact is, many people rely on tips to make up for what are often poor hourly salaries. Therefore, unless service is truly horrendous, you can figure on tipping everyone from bellmen and porters (usually $1 a bag; or $2 if only one bag); to hotel doormen ($2 if they hail you a cab); hotel maids ($2 a day, left in your room when you check out), rest room attendants (at least 50¢), and room-service waiters (approximately 15 percent of the bill unless already added on). In restaurants, the best way to figure out the tip is to double the tax (which adds up to a little more than 16 percent; add or subtract a dollar or two depending on how the service was). In taxis, tip 15 percent of the total fare, with a $2 minimum.

Tourist Information

NYC & Company Visitors Information Center, 810 Seventh Avenue (between West 52nd and 53rd streets); tel: 212-484-1222; www.nycgo.com; Mon–Fri 8.30am– 6pm, Sat–Sun 10am–5pm. The center offers brochures, maps, and information about hotel packages and attraction discounts. An information kiosk is at Broadway and Park Row at City Hall Park.
Times Square Information Center, is at the Embassy Theater, Seventh Ave between 46th and 47th sts, tel: 212-869 1890. It's a source of citywide info, with a ticket counter for shows, email facilities, and ATMs. It's open daily 8am–8pm, with free walking tours. www.timessquarenyc.org.

Transportation

Subways and Buses
Subways and buses run 24 hours a

day, less frequently after midnight, with the fare payable by exact change as well as by MetroCard pass (available at subway ticket booths), which allows free transfers within two hours of use. Unlimited-ride passes good for seven or 30 days are also available, as is a day pass sold at newsstands, hotels, and electronic kiosks in some subway stations. Buses run on most avenues (except Park Avenue between 40th and 120th streets) as well as on the following cross-streets: Houston, 14th, 23rd, 34th, 42nd, 57th, 66th, 86th, 116th, and 125th.

Subway trains cross town at 14th, 42nd, and 53rd streets. There is no north–south line east of Lexington Avenue or west of Eighth Avenue and Broadway above 59th Street.

For general bus and subway information, check www.mta.info or tel: 718-330 1234; for details about MetroCard and other passes, call 212-METROCARD.

PATH Trains
PATH (Port Authority Trans Hudson) trains run under the Hudson River from six stations in Manhattan to Hoboken, Jersey City, and Newark in New Jersey. For more information check www.panynj.gov, tel: 800-234 7284.

Rail and Bus Stations
Long-distance and commuter trains arrive and depart from Manhattan's two railroad terminals: Grand Central Terminal at Park Avenue and 42nd Street, and Pennsylvania Station at Seventh Avenue and 33rd Street. For Amtrak information, tel: 800-872 7245. The city's main bus terminal is the Port Authority (Eighth Avenue between 40th and 42nd streets). The station sits atop two subway lines and is serviced by long-distance bus companies (including Greyhound, tel: 800-231-2222) and local commuter lines. City buses stop outside.

Websites
www.newyork.citysearch.com for listings and reviews of current arts and entertainment events, as well as restaurants and shopping. It's excellent for links to every conceivable aspect of New York City. www.nyc.gov is the official site of the City of New York. It contains news items, mayoral updates, city agency information, and details of parking regulations.
www.nycgo.com is the New York City tourism website, with information on accommodations, restaurants, shopping, upcoming events, and promotional deals.
www.centralparknyc.org has a calendar of events, maps, and other information about Central Park. www.nypl.org is for everything you ever wanted to know about the New York Public Library.

Index

Insight Select Guide: New York
Written by: Stephen Brewer and Mimi Tompkins
Edited by: Cathy Muscat
Layout by: Ian Spick
Maps: James Macdonald
Picture Manager: Steven Lawrence
Series Editor: Cathy Muscat

Photography: Courtesy Ace Hotel 170T; Alamy 49, 50, 75, 125, 140, 159; Courtesy Algonquin Hotel; AMNH/R. Mickens 10T; Becks Studio 76T ; Laura Bittner 14B; Karen Blumberg 4/5, 118; Micheal Bodycomb 8; Courtesy The Carlyle 174M; Chris Chen 7; Click Gallery 129; Courtesy Cooper Square Hotel 106, 170M; Corbis 104, 113; Noelle D'Arrigo 147; Michael Daddino 124; Dan Deluca 90; Daniel 34; Michel Denance/Morgan Library 15; Courtesy Dressing Room Bar & Boutique 134; Stephane Eten 81; Eyevine 16, 37, 80, 119, 120, 138/139; Alberto Di Fabio. Courtesy Gagosian Gallery. Photography by Robert McKeever 32; Steven Freeman 128; Fred George 13T; Courtesy Gramercy Park Hotel 176T; The Frick Collection Michael Bodycomb 35; Cox-Goldberg Photography, Inc 33; Getty Images 38/39, 100, 101, 112; Goodrob 136; Courtesy H&H Bagels 28; Courtesy The Hotel Excelsior 177T; Courtesy Hotel on Rivington 170B; Courtesy The Inn at Irving 173T; Keiki Niwa 130, 146; APA Abe Nowitz 10B, 19, 22, 29, 53, 54, 68, 76, 82, 88, 108, 110, 114B, 122/123, 156, 157, 165, 166, 174B; NY Flyer 98; APA Richard Nowitz 56B, 152/153, 154, 163; PA Photos 30; Petter Palander 109; Paula Court 70/71; Eduardo Pavon 126; Peninsula Hotels 60; Photolibrary 10B, 51; Courtesy Pod Hotel 168/169, 179T; Prospect Park Alliance 160/161B; Robert Polidori for the Skyscraper Museum 148; Courtesy The Royalton 172M; Courtesy the Russian Baths 141; Scala 31; June Shieh 145; Ellen Silverman 89; The Skyscraper Museum Archive 163; Courtesy The Soho Grand 176B; Starwood Hotels 172B; Leo Sorel 158; APA Chris Stowers 91; Superstock 8, 73, 142; Sunghwan Yoon 52; Courtesy St Regis Hotel 69, 175T; TIPS Images 11; Voices of Ascension 107; Courtesy Waldorf Astoria 175M; Charlie K Walker 137; Courtesy

Washington Square Hotel 179B; Marcin Wichary 3T, 160/161; Ed Yourdon 6, 36, 105, 177C; Garrett Ziegler 87, 99

First Edition 2010, Reprinted 2011
© 2010 Apa Publications GmbH & Co.
Verlag KG Singapore Branch, Singapore.
Printed in Germany

Contacting the Editors
We would appreciate it if readers would alert us to outdated information by writing to:
Apa Publications, PO Box 7910, London SE1 1WE, UK; email: insight@apaguide.co.uk

Distribution:
Distributed in the UK and Ireland by:
GeoCenter International Ltd
Meridian House, Churchill Way West, Basingstoke, Hampshire RG21 6YR; tel: (44 1256) 817 987; email: sales@geocenter.co.uk
Distributed in the United States by:
Ingram Publisher Services
One Ingram Blvd, PO Box 3006, La Vergne, TN 37086-1986; email: customer.service@ingrampublisherservices.com
Distributed in Australia by:
Universal Publishers
PO Box 307, St. Leonards, NSW 1590;
email: sales@universalpublishers.com.au
Distributed in New Zealand by:
Hema Maps New Zealand Ltd (HNZ)
Unit 2, 10 Cryers Road, East Tamaki, Auckland 2013; email: sales.hema@clear.net.nz
Worldwide distribution by:
Apa Publications GmbH & Co. Verlag KG
Singapore, 7030 Ang Mo Kio Ave 5, 08-65 Northstar @ AMK, Singapore 569880; tel: (65) 6570 1051; email: apasin@singnet.com.sg